Secrets of Résumés and Application Letters that Work

Secrets of Résumés and Application Letters that Work

Strategies for Creating Materials that Stand Out & Land Interviews

Caroline M. Cole, Ph.D.

Ethos Professional Communication
www.ethosprofessionalcommunication.com

Secrets of Résumés and Application Letters that Work
ISBN 13: 978-0-9981387-0-1 | ISBN 10: 0-9981387-0-3

Dedication

for my mother, Grace, who taught me
to believe that we are capable of
doing anything we set our hearts and minds to

and

for my students over the years,
who have and continue
to challenge and inspire me with their questions

Contents

Introduction x

Part 1: Getting Started

Secret 1, Assessment 14

Exercise: Fast-forward… 17

Exercise: "Top 5" Standouts 20

Exercise: Rankings 20

Exercise: Career Possibilities 21

Exercise: Current Awareness Levels (CALs) 22

Exercise: Moving Dreams Into Reality 24

Secret 2, Focus 27

Exercise: Ideal Employer Profile 28

Exercise: Ideal Employee Profile 32

Exercise: Mash Up 33

Secret 3, Time 36

Exercise: The 10-Second Review 38

Secret 4, Purpose 40

Secret 5, Audience 42

Secret 6 , Leverage 43

Part 2: Résumés

Secret 7, Content 47

Exercise: Résumé Content Review 59

Secret 8, Performance 60

Exercise: Tightening Résumé Descriptors 64

Secret 9, Substance 65

Exercise: Résumé Show or Tell? 75

Secret 10, Type 76

Exercise: Generating Your Master Résumé File 83

Exercise: Switching Formats and Increasing Options 85

Secret 11, Bullets 86

Exercise: Bullets to Paragraphs, and Vice Versa 90

Secret 12, Signposts 94

Exercise: Making a Strong First Impression 103

Exercise: Tracking the Reader's Gaze 105

Exercise: Tightening the Dangling Elements 107

Secret 13, Format 108

Exercise: Making Conscientious Format Choices 109

Exercise: Going on Record 113

Part 3: Application Letters

Secret 14, Personalization 119

Exercise: The Salutation Test 120

Exercise: Spotting The "Plug-n-Chug" Application Letter 122

Secret 15, Structure 123

Secret 16, Openings 126

Exercise: Creating a Company-Specific Opening Paragraph 130

Secret 17, Ego 132

Exercise: The "I's" Have It… 133

Exercise: The "I's" Have It …, Variation 134

Exercise: First Impressions 136

Exercise: What Color Dominates? 142

Secret 18, Emphasis 143

Exercise: Creating a You–Me–Us Brainstorming Chart 149

Exercise: Generating "You–Me–Us" Paragraphs 156

Secret 19, Hype 159

Exercise: Application Letter Show or Tell? 163

Secret 20, Closings 165

Exercise: Creating a Concise, Action-Oriented Closing Paragraphs 171

Exercise: Bringing It All Together 174

Final Notes… 175

Exercise: The $50k Investment Test 176

Introduction

As jobs remain scarce, employers stay selective about the applicants they interview. There are, however, ways a résumé and application letter can set you apart from other applicants—if you know what to do.

If you're reading this guide, chances are you're entering the workforce, between positions, or looking to change jobs… and, perhaps, you've been finding today's market is less accessible or accommodating than ideal. If so, you're not alone. Unfortunately, the overwhelming number of resources offering varying lists of do's and don'ts regarding résumés and application letters make it harder for even the most earnest job seekers to know which advice to follow in general, and which advice will help their application materials stand out. More unfortunate is that information overload is only part of the problem.

Offering prescriptive rules and ready-to-apply suggestions, job search advice often strips away contextualizing elements that help applicants understand why some strategies may work, why others may not, and why the success of most strategies ultimately depends on the context. In essence, these materials omit critical information that could help job applicants make better, more informed choices as they create or revise their résumés and application letters. This book is different.

Secrets of Résumés and Application Letters that Work examines secrets of successful résumés and application letters, yet while the word "secrets" suggests this guide will present gimmicks job applicants can use to trick prospective employers into considering their application, nothing could be further from the truth. Certainly there are applicants who misrepresent their skills and abilities during a job search in general, and in résumés and application letters in particular, but such deception serves neither employers, nor applicants in the long run. Therefore, rather than support superficial razzle-dazzle, this guide advocates and offers a framework of credible practices to highlight your experiences and capabilities to organizations that interest you.

The principles and strategies outlined in this book may be little known and, thus, little used, but they aren't secret. They're time-tested practices of effective communication. Still, the fact that so few application materials reflect these principles validates the need for a guide that explains what these practices are, and how they can be invaluable in the context of a job search.

This book starts with secrets that can help you identify and target positions and opportunities that best match your talents and interests. It then discusses the expectations hiring managers often use to evaluate job applicants, further contextualizing the secrets about résumés and application letters, both individually and collectively.

Chances are, you already have a résumé, but want to ensure it gets the strongest consideration. The secrets in this section explain how you can identify, situate, and highlight information in your résumé in ways that appeal to hiring managers.

Secrets about application letters wrap up the guide. Although many jobs may not require an application letter, the information in this section can help you stand out when application letters are possible. And should you decide *not* to submit an application letter, the secrets in this section can help you prepare for interviews.

Throughout this book, you will find step-by-step exercises to help you generate more effective, competitive job application documents. These activities require time—certainly more time than the "plug-n'-chug" application materials that dominate the market. Therefore, if you don't have the time, energy, or interest to invest in something you hope to do for the next year or more, you may not be ready to do it. Similiarly, if you're seeking easy answers and instant results, this book is not for you.

If, however, you're willing to approach each discussion in good faith and complete the corresponding exercises with care, you will find ways to discuss your talents with greater precision, clarity, and conviction, and do so in ways that get the attention of hiring managers.

In picking up this material, you demonstrate that you're not only wanting to set yourself apart, but that you're willing to take concrete steps to do so. My hope is that by reading this book and completing its exercises, you will find ways to identify, articulate, and showcase your talents and, in turn, land interviews with companies that value your abilities.

Part 1

Getting Started

Secret 1: Career assessment is valuable at any stage of a career, helping individuals identify (or verify) what they want to do and why, so they can convince others to pay them to do it.

Lewis Carroll's *Alice's Adventures in Wonderland* focuses on Alice who, following a mysterious White Rabbit down a rabbit hole under the hedge, enters "Wonderland," a fantastical world inhabited by many strange characters, such as the March Hare, Mad Hatter, the King and Queen of Hearts, and the Cheshire Cat. Although Carroll's story may seem to have little relevance to those launching a job search, the way many people look for jobs may reveal more similarities than differences.

There is, for example, the effect of impulsively, haphazardly, and uncritically chasing people, things, illusions, and so on that catch our eye. People may have moved through school, positions, companies, and even careers in such a manner that, upon reflection, they find they have tumbled into an absurd and unfamiliar world peppered with characters they consider unusual, eccentric, and even a bit frightening.

Trying to adjust to their new environments, they may inevitably discover the instability of their own—and others'—identity. Along the way, they may encounter rules, social norms, and expectations that defy everything they have known to date. The naïve would dismiss these conventions as silly, yet eliminating them completely would be as dangerous as upholding them blindly.

Ultimately, it's a person's ability to manage situations that seem controlled by inconsistent, arbitrary policies that leads to success. The twists and turns required to move through unfamiliar and, at times, confusing places are ever-present and ever-uncertain, especially in the workplace. Choices may not be choices *per se*, but reactions to known and unknown forces, leading to greater anxieties. And while there may be moments of calm or even clarity, those moments may be short-lived and quickly undermined by the next, unexpected encounter, just like Alice found.

Alice's Adventures in Wonderland documents a wonderful journey, but it also offers a cautionary tale about letting others lead us on paths that can make us unsure of who we are, what we want, or if we truly belong in the places we land. Career assessment aims to mitigate these dangers by helping us thoughtfully examine our values, talents, and interests so that we might discover work that would engage our best selves, find forums to support our efforts, and pursue those opportunities with passion.

To help in this endeavor, we turn to a question that is often asked of children: "What do you want to be when you grow up?"

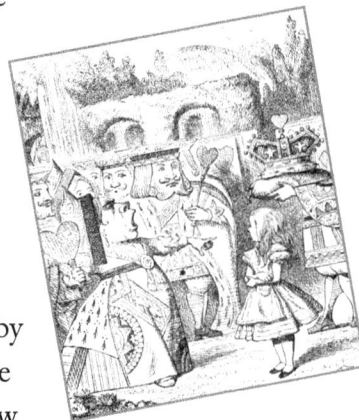

As a child and, perhaps, even as an adult, you may have envisioned yourself in a particular field or position that, to date, remains elusive. Or, possibly, you're on the way to achieving your dream job, but need guidance navigating the intermediate steps. Maybe you've found a career by default, rather than by choice, and wonder if there could be something more for you if you only knew what those alternatives were. Perhaps you have experienced detours that have not only moved you further from your target destination, but left you unsure about how to find your way back on course. Or maybe you're struggling to develop a strategy for leaving a familiar and safe, but mundane job—especially in today's economy—in search of a position that engages your talents and stimulates your interests. It's also possible you have reached the position you thought you wanted only to learn it wasn't for you after all.

Career aspirations change—sometimes unconsciously. Therefore, all successful job searches should include opportunities to identify or validate career options that both excite and inspire you. Because guided daydreaming can help identify personal and professional ambitions, the following exercises provide an occasion to consider work and forums that match your interests and talents, helping you to decide where and how to move forward.

Although you can do these exercises in isolation, you should aim to complete at least the first three exercises together to build upon the momentum.

Exercise: Fast-forward…

Set a timer for 10–15 minutes and let your mind drift to the first day on the job of your ideal career or position, whatever you define it to be. Envision the day from start to finish, thinking less about a specific organization you'd like to work with and more about the people, the environment, the tasks that would give you pleasure. Consider, for example…

what time does your day begin…

what clothes do you put on as you get ready to go to work…

what activities do you do prior to leaving for work…

how do you get to work, and what is the commute like…

what do you find and whom do you encounter when you first arrive at your place of business…

what is the first thing you do as you settle into your work for the day…

what types of things do you do as you move through the day…

what questions and concerns do you encounter, what types of problems do you solve, what needs do you fulfill…

with whom do you meet throughout the day, and what types of interactions do you have…

how do you feel during those encounters…

what people and resources are necessary to ensure the success of your various endeavors, and where, how, and with what effort are you able to engage with or otherwise secure those resources…

what will be the signs or measurements of success in your various enterprises, and who (or what) gets to decide those criteria…

when and how does your day wrap up…

what's the reverse commute like…

who or what awaits you upon your return home…
what work needs to be done before you can relax or retire…
and, finally, what time does your day actually end?

Engage all of your senses as you think about "doing" your profession and your work, creating a forum that you could actively and enthusiastically think about, participate in, and contribute to—every day, if necessary—regardless of how much you are paid.

If it helps, use the space on the next page to jot down notes or key words that come to mind. If you're feeling artistic, sketch out possibilities or use images from magazines to create a collage of elements you'd like to have in your professional world.

My ideal career or position would entail…

words, ideas that come to mind

images that reflect my ideal work

Exercise: "Top 5" Standouts

Set the timer for another 5–10 minutes and, as quickly as possible, identify the top five images, ideas, details, characteristics… that stand out as the most appealing for you from the "Fast-Forward…" exercise. The items you list might include people, projects, venues, opportunities, or any combination of these elements.

❶ __________

❷ __________

❸ __________

❹ __________

❺ __________

Exercise: Rankings

Set the timer for another 5 minutes and, as quickly as possible, *rank* the items you listed in the "Top 5 Standouts" exercise from the most important (1) in your ideal job to the least important (5):

❶ __________

❷ __________

❸ __________

❹ __________

❺ __________

Exercise: Career Possibilities

Using the information that came to mind as you thought about your ideal position and ranked elements of greatest importance to you, use the space below to list careers, industries, companies and positions that might accommodate and value these interests as you envisioned them. For assistance or additional inspiration, enter some of the words and ideas that came to mind into a search engine or into the search option of an online job announcement databank to see what kinds of positions bring together these elements.

Exercise: Current Awareness Levels (CALs)

Using the information you identified in the "Career Possibilities" exercise, consider the fields and industries where this work is done, companies that value this work, positions that do this work, and the skills employees need to do this work efficiently. Then, in the following chart, record what you *currently* know about these fields, companies, positions…, what you *don't* know, and what you *could* know if you were to talk with people, research the work or position online, and so on. Use additional paper as necessary.

Current Awareness Levels (CALs)

Element	What/Whom I *DO* know…	What/Whom I *DON'T* know…	What/Whom I *COULD* know…
fields and industries that value this work			
top companies doing this work			
possible position(s) or job(s) that would allow me to do this work			
expectations of the employees holding these positions or doing this work (e.g., degrees, training, skill sets)			
individuals doing this work			

Exercise: Moving Dreams Into Reality

Now that you've identified contexts and opportunities that may be of interest, list *specific* actions you can take in the next 6, 12, 18 and 24 months to complete, update, and build upon the areas you identified in the "Current Awareness Levels (CALs)" exercise. Be as specific as possible, breaking larger, abstract tasks into several smaller, concrete ones if necessary. For example:

Read 10 job descriptions concerning *Position X* each week, identifying and comparing company expectations for employees doing the work that interests me

Do a skills assessment of what I presently have and what I must develop to be competitive in this area

Meet with five people in my immediate circle to brainstorm ways to…

Go to a career fair to talk with…

Research different organizations that offer positions that support work in…

Ask five friends for contacts they may have in the field of…

Arrange an informational interview to discuss…

Attend a networking event to meet…

Read about one company in my target field each week to learn more about…

Make appointment with current supervisor to discuss…

Participate in online discussion forums with others who…

Look for local course, workshop, or training opportunity to learn or update skills in [insert skill(s)]…

Now create your Personal Plan of Action by identifying specific actions you can take in the next 6, 12, 18, and 24 months.

Actions to take in the next…

…6 months

❶ ______

❷ ______

❸ ______

❹ ______

❺ ______

…12 months

❶ ______

❷ ______

❸ ______

❹ ______

❺ ______

…18 months

❶ ______

❷ ______

❸ ______

❹ ______

❺ ______

...24 months

❶ ______________________________

❷ ______________________________

❸ ______________________________

❹ ______________________________

❺ ______________________________

Congratulations! In completing these exercises, you have identified and narrowed possibilities that will make your search easier and more focused on finding opportunities that can bring you closer to your dream position. This information will also help you revise and develop your application materials to apply for such positions, as we'll discuss in the following secrets.

* * *

Before discussing secrets that directly affect application materials, a word on this book's use of "hiring manager."

Every company—whether it's a sole-proprietorship or a corporation with offices around the globe—has its own structure and process for hiring team members and, by extension, titles for those working with prospective employees and their files. In some cases, it may be a manager or director in the specific division needing more assistance. In other cases it may be members of the organization's Human Resources department. In a startup, it may be the CEO. Given the range of possibilities, this book uses the term "hiring manager" to simplify and streamline references to the individuals who may recruit applicants, review and screen applications, interview candidates, and help bring job searches to a successful conclusion.

So, with that, we turn to more secrets...

Secret 2: Applicants are not the primary focus of a job search.

Most applicants look for jobs with their interests in mind: What kind of work do they want to do? What company would they like to work for? What kind of people do they want around them? How much money will make the work worthwhile to them? Such questions can help applicants find and narrow positions of interest, but they also have a tendency to obscure the most important character in the story, at least according to the people making the ultimate decision: the employer.

Hiring managers know why people submit applications for the jobs they're advertising. Applicants want a paycheck, they want the status of having the company's name on their résumé, they want an opportunity to move one step closer to their dream job.... Any one of these reasons—or even all of them—could bring top-notch candidates to the applicant pool, but none of them matter to hiring managers who are mostly concerned with what *they* will get from the hire.

Hiring managers generally look for two things in an applicant: someone who can help *the company* make more money, and someone who can help *them* look good in front of management so *they* can make more money. Certainly hiring managers need to make sure that the prospective applicants are likable, that they can play nice, and that others in the office would want to work with them; that's what the interview is for. But to get an interview, applicants must demonstrate that they can make the company and the hiring manager look good.

Recognizing that you and a hiring manager will view your application materials differently can help you contextualize and frame your experiences to appeal to the audiences you want to reach: companies wanting to hire reliable, competent individuals.

The following exercises can help you identify concerns that may be of greatest interest to the hiring managers reading your materials and, ultimately, deciding whether to advance your application.

Exercise: Ideal Employer Profile

In the earlier career assessment exercises, you envisioned your ideal position and, perhaps, the tasks you'd be doing, the people you'd be working with, the setting you'd be doing it in, and so on. Assuming that your ideal position is *not* self-employment, for now you're going to put youself on the other side of the interview table and imagine that you are the person in charge of hiring employees for your ideal position. In other words, you're going to play the role of hiring manager.

Playing the role of hiring manager, think about the education and training you would have gotten to prepare for this position, the work you would have done up to this point in your career, the experiences you've gained, the years you have put in, and the reputation you've both earned and now want to protect. Record ideas that come to mind:

____

____

____

____

____

____

____

____

____

____

____

____

Now, think about the work that needs to be done in the weeks, months, and years ahead in order to meet the short- and long-term goals that you or your office has set, to avoid or minimize loss (e.g., time, money, quality, reputation), to get the salary or bonuses you seek, to remain competitive in the office or industry. . . . Record ideas that come to mind:

Next, think about the types of people you want on your team to help with that work. Think about the people who would be working with you, or even alongside you, sometimes for hours at a time. Think about the individuals you would want and need to depend on to get the work done when and as necessary. Think about those who would help the company do well, but also help you look good to your supervisors and among your colleagues. Now, consider that you want to hire *the best* person from among the possibilities …

What education, training, or experience would be mandatory for the person you would need and want to hire, and why?

What experiences would be highly desirable, and why?

What training and experience would be nice to have, and why?

What education, training, and experience would help this person start doing the work immediately, saving you time on training and oversight?

For any training that would be necessary, what characteristics would make that work easiest for you?

What skills, training, experiences, and so on would give this new hire an advantage in the work he or she would be doing in the short and long term—and in what ways?

What skills and interests would your ideal applicants have to make them more effective and efficient in their primary and secondary responsibilities?

What would you consider to be bonus skills and experiences for the most competitive applicant, and why?

Take 15–20 minutes to list the training, experiences, characteristics of the best type of employee for this work—someone who could both complete the work that needs to be done *and* help you build your own reputation and image within the organization; use additional paper, as necessary. If you get stuck, look at job announcements for positions in the industry to see how companies package their requests for employees.

Exercise: Ideal Employee Profile

Now that you have identified things your Ideal Employer might want, value, and need in an ideal employee, take 15–20 minutes to list the education, training, experience, characteristics *you* have to match those expectations, satisfy those needs, and meet those challenges; use additional paper as necessary. If you get stuck, look at your current résumé, or earlier versions of your résumé, and other application materials you've used to generate ideas.

Exercise: Mash Up

In reviewing the lists you generated for the "Ideal Employer Profile" and the "Ideal Employee Profile," you might begin to see places these lists overlap. List items that appear on *both* lists in the overlapping area of the circles below.

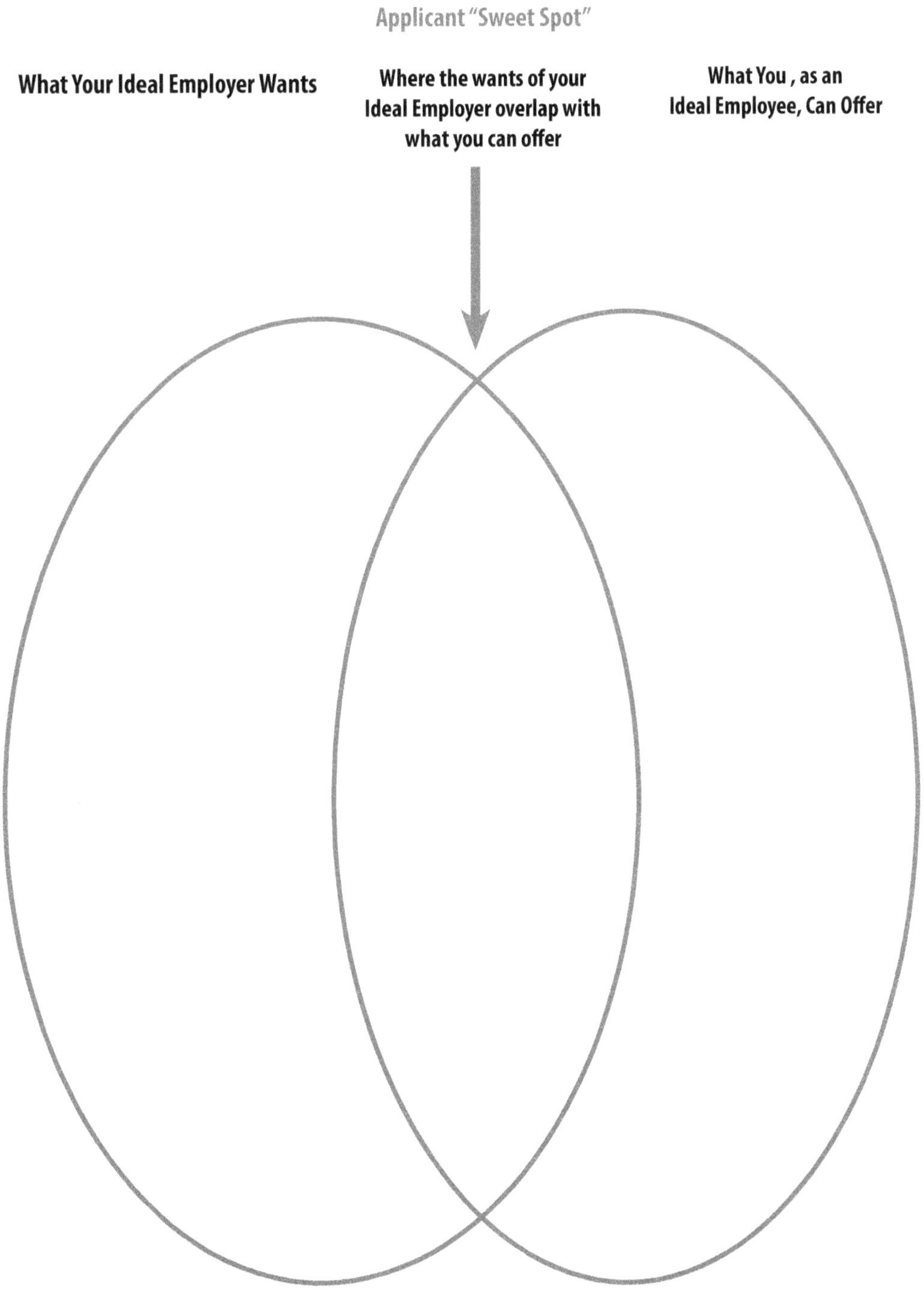

Applicant "Sweet Spot"

What Your Ideal Employer Wants

Where the wants of your Ideal Employer overlap with what you can offer

What You , as an Ideal Employee, Can Offer

The place where the circles overlap represents the "Applicant Sweet Spot," characteristics both a hiring manager for your dream position would want *and* you can presently offer.

In later sections, we'll examine how you can highlight this information in application materials but, for now, we're going to focus on where the circles do *not* overlap.

What Your *Ideal Employer* Wants, Highlights

Review the elements that remain solely in the "What Your Ideal Employer Would Want" circle and record the top three skills or abilities your Ideal Employer would expect to find in the most competitive applicants:

❶ ______________________________

❷ ______________________________

❸ ______________________________

Next, identify tangible ways you could begin to acquire or strengthen these skills and abilities in the weeks, months, or years ahead.

❶ ______________________________

❷ ______________________________

❸ ______________________________

Although you might not be able to develop full proficiency or expertise in any or all of the areas *before* you apply for a job, starting to learn or strengthen these skills and abilities would let you discuss ways you are working to fill in potential gaps, making you more viable for positions that require these traits.

What *You* Can Offer, Highlights

Review the elements that remain solely in the "What You Can Offer" circle and record the top three skills or abilities you can offer your Ideal Employer in the space below.

1. ____________________
2. ____________________
3. ____________________

Now, identify tangible ways your Ideal Employer could put these experiences to use in both the work that needs to be done *and* in the way that your Ideal Employer would do it.

These items may be details to address in a résumé, application letter, or even during an interview, as we'll discuss in the following pages.

Secret 3: Applicants over-estimate the time employers spend reading résumés and application letters.

Ask job applicants how much time they think hiring managers spend reading an application, and the answers are all over the place: 7–10 minutes… 2½ minutes… 5 minutes… 60 seconds… While the numbers people toss out may reflect wishing thinking, the realty is that hiring managers average 5–10 seconds on any one application, highlighting the arbitrary, subjective, and even whimsical approach hiring managers might use when reviewing applications.

Some hiring managers, for example, dismiss applications outright if they're printed on a particular color paper, or because the typeface is too small, or because the content is too scattered. Others breeze through application materials looking for a particular detail that, when found, determines whether the application moves forward or gets tossed into the recycle bin. And as more companies adopt online Application Tracking Systems, key-word filters and auto-sorting software cull a majority of applications before they're seen by a person. Each of these methods requires only a second or two.

Although some applicants may be outraged to learn that their documents get little more than a passing glance, here context can be valuable. Whereas people used to spend hours crafting and submitting materials to a handful of organizations, computers now allow applicants to write a single letter and respond to hundreds of job announcements with a few keystrokes, overwhelming companies with minimally qualified applicants who have decided to apply as broadly as possible with the hopes that *something* will materialize.

Companies are fighting back with technology that ruthlessly sorts and cuts applicants, making hiring decisions faster and easier. Yet even organizations that don't use applicant-screening software and comparable systems look for reasons to eliminate applicants quickly so they can make the necessary offers, close the search, and move on. In such a context, hiring managers argue that a cursory look at applications is sufficient.

The good news is that hiring managers *average* 5–10 seconds on each document, so while some applications get a split-second of attention, others will get more time—much more time. And, while it may not be possible to know what criteria each company uses to rule out an applicant, there are ways to increase the chances that your materials will be among those getting a more thoughtful review.

We'll examine some of those ways in the coming discussions, but understanding that prospective employers may not spend the amount of time you think—or hope—your materials deserve can encourage more strategic decisions both in what you decide to present, and how.

Exercise: The 10-Second Review

For this exercise, you need a hard copy of your application materials (a résumé, application letter, or both) and a volunteer reviewer who has not seen these materials, or seen them recently.

Step 1: Set a timer for 10 seconds (or, if you're feeling generous, 15 seconds)

Step 2: Give the reviewer the following instructions: *"I'm going to give you my [résumé and/or application letter] and ask that you digest as much information as possible about my credentials in an undisclosed amount of time."*

Step 3: Hand your materials to your reviewer and start the timer.

When the timer goes off, ask the reviewer the following questions and record the answers in the space below:

What attracted your attention?

Where did your eyes focus first, second, third…?

What details stood out most, and why?

What do you recall most easily from the materials you saw?

____

____

____

____

____

____

____

____

For variation, repeat this exercise with another volunteer or two to see if, and where, there is overlap in what the readers notice.

The information you get from the volunteer reviewer(s) can help you identify which details and information in your application materials are attracting attention, helping you decide whether such information serves your purpose.

Secret 4: Applicants who know and leverage the purpose of application materials can make better decisions about what details to include—and exclude—within these materials.

In creating or updating their résumés and application letters, applicants inevitably have questions: Is there information that's mandatory to provide, regardless of the position they may be seeking? Do they have to list every job they've held—even the menial ones, or work they didn't like and, therefore, would never want to do again? Should they mention that they were let go from a particular position? What if they haven't held a job for several months, or even several years? What if they've changed jobs often?

Should recent graduates provide their GPAs and, if so, when should they stop including it? When can they remove experiences or details from their résumé and not be penalized? Is it possible to give too much or too little information? Are there ways to focus descriptions without becoming so narrow and precise that they actually typecast the applicant, thereby limiting subsequent opportunities? What do hiring managers notice and value most in the applications they see? What are the best ways to help their materials stand out from the rest?…

Such questions suggest that applicants want to know how to present themselves and their circumstances in the most strategic manner to prospective employers. But to answer these and countless other questions about résumé and application letter content, we must know the purpose of these documents.

Most applicants think they submit résumés and application letters to get a job. They do not. They submit these materials to get an *interview*, and they go on interview(s) to get the job.

It's a subtle, but critical difference, and one that's vital when considering what information to give companies, and when.

For example, some information may be understandable with context that isn't always possible—or appropriate—to give on a résumé or in an application letter, but the only way applicants could strategically provide that information is to get their foot in the door. Therefore, by knowing when and how to disclose information, you can build a stronger case for employment.

There is, however, a caveat to this secret: Applicants must be willing and prepared to disclose all job-related information, even that which may be unflattering. In other words, delaying the presentation of information is not the same thing as avoiding, hiding, or otherwise misrepresenting potentially problematic information; it's simply a matter of choosing *when* to reveal it, if you have the option to decide.

If, for example, a job announcement requires particular information in applicant materials, you may need to provide that information up front—especially in, say, online applications that require specific information before the system will accept the submission. If, however, you have flexibility in the information you provide in the initial application materials, you might be able to postpone the discussion of some details until you can offer more context and commentary.

The following discussions examine ways to present information in the most strategic manner, but understanding the purpose of materials at each stage in the job search process can help you make better choices about what information to present, and when, to strengthen your application for a job.

Secret 5: Applicants who know the audiences of particular application materials can be more strategic in presenting their credentials in ways that matter.

Application materials target prospective employers, but résumés and application letters actually have different audiences. Understanding the differences can affect the information applicants provide and, by extension, the case they are able to make for employment.

Résumés are *industry* specific, allowing applicants to submit the same résumé to multiple companies with comparable job openings. In contrast, application letters are unique to the particular organization. Application letters may draw upon and highlight details from the applicant's résumé; moreover, the letter an applicant sends to one company may have elements that overlap with letters the applicant sends to different companies with comparable positions. *Each* letter, however, should be unique, explaining how, why, and to what extent the applicant fits the particular position, as the particular organization has envisioned it. This distinction is one that few applicants make—often to their detriment.

By understanding that résumés and application letters have specific audiences, you can use these document individually and in tandem to attract the attention of hiring managers in the companies that appeal most to you.

Secret 6: Applicants who understand Secrets 4 & 5 get more space to demonstrate their qualifications for the positions they seek.

Job applicants often complain that they "have only one page" to convey substantial experience to a prospective employer when, in fact, they may have *two* pages to make their case for employment: an industry-specific résumé and a company-specific application letter. Yet while all applicants may have the same amount of space to explain their qualifications for a particular position, the ways applicants use that space can make a difference in the case they are able to make.

Résumés, for instance, offer hiring managers a synopsis of an applicant's professional experiences and abilities in the larger industry. What may not be clear, however, is where and how that expertise could transfer to the hiring manager's specific organization. That's where an application letter comes into play. Specifically, the application letter would highlight information from the applicant's résumé to help the hiring manager understand how a particular combination of experience has prepared the individual to do the work the company wants done.

Certainly the résumé and the application letter will draw upon the same information, but keeping each document's distinct purpose and audience in mind can help you strategically coordinate these documents' content to demonstrate how you are a match for the specific opening.

* * *

The following sections examine ways to incorporate these secrets into résumés and application letters that convey your talents and abilities in ways that appeal to hiring managers.

Part 2

Résumés

As noted earlier, résumés are *industry* specific, allowing applicants to submit the same résumé to multiple companies with comparable job openings. Yet, recognizing that some positions may require unique expectations in a particular forum, savvy job hunters have more than one type of résumé and, perhaps, multiple versions of each type to highlight context-specific expertise.

Regardless of how many résumés they may have, applicants should be aware of characteristics in a résumé that can immediately discredit or dismiss even the most qualified individuals. Certainly recruiters and head hunters have personal preferences and biases when reviewing an applicant's materials, but hiring managers generally agree that résumés with the following characteristics can damage the applicant's chances to secure an interview:

Too long. Résumés should offer an abridged synopsis of the applicant's qualifications. Although some individuals insist on using résumés with two or more pages, such résumés may receive minimal attention, especially if hiring managers find information on the résumé they consider unnecessary.

Disorganized. Résumés should be organized and laid out in ways that help readers find main categories and key details within seconds.

Poorly designed, formatted, or printed. Résumés should adopt reader-friendly typefaces, font sizes, line spacing, margins, and printout quality so information is easy to find, read, reproduce and, if necessary, forward.

Too sparse. Résumés should indicate what an applicant has done in concrete, tangible terms, rather than assume that company names, titles, abbreviated job descriptions, industry jargon, and so on are self-explanatory.

Overwritten. Résumés should provide detailed, yet concise descriptions of the applicant's credentials; taking too long to say too little can suggest artificially inflated experience, inefficiency, arrogance, or worse.

Not results-oriented. Résumés should move beyond listing duties and tasks the applicant has been responsible for and explain the value of the applicants' work to the organization.

Irrelevance-laden. Résumés should highlight the training, skills, and experiences that qualify the applicant for a position, rather than information that gives prospective employers a means to discriminate against applicants (e.g., height, weight, opportunities not taken).

Superficially appealing. Résumés should resist using fancy (or multiple) typefaces, ink color, paper stock, and so forth to attract attention and, instead, convey reader-oriented credentials.

Incoherent, inaccurate, ungrammatical. Résumés should present an applicant's technical qualifications for a position, as well as the applicant's competency in general workplace practices (e.g., clarity of expression, attention to details, conventional language use).

Misdirected. Résumés should target audiences that work with application materials on a permanent or *ad hoc* basis, rather than generic readers (e.g., To Whom it May Concern, or Dear Sir or Madam), inappropriate staff members (e.g., CEOs that don't read first-round applications), or company divisions with no apparent link to the applicant's training.

Addressing these and other concerns hiring managers have about résumés, the secrets that follow offer strategies for generating precise, concise descriptions of your experiences in ways that stand out to hiring managers.

Secret 7: There is information résumés should always include, never include, and might include—depending on the job applicant's circumstances.

Although we expect, or assume, that companies hire the most qualified individual(s) from among all the applications they receive, the hiring process is more subjective than we might hope. Therefore, applicants must be attentive to the information they present on their résumé, and the information they should offer at a later point, if at all.

Information résumés should *always* include...

Résumés should provide information that allows a hiring manager to see and infer your experience, competency, and success, but it's not enough that you say you can do the job; you must must help the hiring manager know you can succeed in the position—a task that is easier when you provide details highlighting your abilities to perform the position's requirement, solve problems, save time, save money, and bring value to the organization. To that end, your résumé should include your:

formal education and training,

professional experiences and accomplishments,

skills that (directly and indirectly) qualify you for the position,

experiences that demonstrate you can work with others in professional forums, and

information that fills in gaps and accounts for time between jobs, if any.

In brief, you need to include details that demonstrate that you can "do the profession" as the industry in general and, perhaps, as the company in particular does it.

Information résumés should *never* include…

Title VII of the Civil Rights Act of 1964 and its various amendments (often known as Equal Employment Opportunity laws) aim to eliminate biased hiring practices in the United States, and reputable companies may have additional formal and informal mechanisms to minimize bias hiring. Still, even the most ethical companies and individuals introduce biases into the hiring process when they evaluate applicants through their lenses, looking for someone they find appealing. Therefore, applicants should be attentive to materials that reveal the following information about themselves in pre-employment forums, including a résumé:

height

weight

age

race

national origin

languages (especially when identifying native fluency)

political party affiliation

religion

disability

sexual orientation

marital status

pregnancy

children

Although most of these categories are protected by equal employment opportunity laws in the United States, others are not. Furthermore, even if companies are *legally* prohibited from using these elements when evaluating prospective employees, individuals reviewing applications may use applicant-provided descriptions in their decisions, even unconsciously. The challenge, of course, is that omitting or minimizing references to these details is easier said than done—especially when training and experience that demonstrate an applicant's qualifications may also disclose information companies could use to discriminate against that applicant; for example, organizations, clubs, societies, and activities may suggest the applicant's race, sex, national origin, religion, political or social views, and so on. Understanding that some hiring decisions could be adversely affected by this information's appearance on your résumé can help you decide when, how, or even if to provide such information before you are offered a position.

Other considerations in this category include photographs of the applicant—a practice that has been discontinued in most forums, but still emerges in contexts requiring applicant identification materials. Finally, although not considered protected status categories, *salary history* and *references* should be omitted from pre-employment documents. Seemingly harmless, salary histories can stereotype you as either over- or under-qualified for a particular position, while references can evoke biases by signaling whether you move within the "right" circles. You should still prepare to provide and discuss this information—say during salary negotiations or other interview segments—but, ideally, these forums will allow you to contextualize and discuss the details in ways that work in your favor.

Information résumés *might* include, depending on the circumstances...

Given the discussions of what to include, and what not to include, applicants are in a better position to decide if and when they might provide the following:

hobbies and interests

social media presence, including blog information

groups and organizations indicating socio-economic, political, religious... affiliations

information found through Google and other employer-friendly search engines

Depending on the context, some employers are using these details in their hiring decisions, in both favorable and unfavorable ways. Applicants who have experience using various social-media outlets, for instance, may be highly desirable to companies immersed in or wanting to develop online communities; those same applicants could be damaging in contexts valuing discretion and privacy.

Online presence likewise gives hiring managers more information (e.g., social media accounts, online photos, blog posts, Tweets) to determine whether an applicant reflects the image and demonstrates the values the company seeks to promote. Knowing that companies could use such information in deciding whether to interview or hire applicants can help you make more conscientious, strategic decisions about what to include and exclude from your preliminary application documents to make the most favorable, professional impression.

* * *

The following secrets assume that you already have a résumé that you are wanting to improve, rather than creating a résumé for the first time. Still, considering the number of resources that offer rigid guidelines on what a résumé should include, the chart below summarizes the most common résumé categories, as well as guidelines and considerations for each category.

The fact that information appears in this chart neither means to suggest that it must appear on every résumé, nor that its inclusion (or exclusion) will have any particular impact on the reception a résumé gets. Instead, the chart simply offers guidelines and considerations for conventional résumé categories so you can decide whether the inclusion of comparable information on your résumé could help convey your experiences to the companies that interest you.

Conventional Résumé Categories

Category	Guidelines and Consideration	Examples
Name	Full, professional name Because names should correspond with academic, employment, government… records, applicants might include references to informal names to help cross-reference other application materials.	THOMAS B. SNYDER Mary Pauline O'Hara, Ph.D. Andrzejek "Andrew" Bieda Xiaodan (see-ow-dah-n) Wang

Category	Guidelines and Consideration	Examples
Contact Information	Full mailing address Phone (no need to distinguish between cellular and landline) E-mail? Website? Blogs? (consider pros and cons)	123 Main St., Apt. 302 | Stockton, CA 95202 (510) 555-1313 | jdoe@gmail.com | dailyeconblogspot.com 789 S. 52nd Street, #870 New York, NY 10003 (212) 555.1212 • c.b.taylor@aol.com
Objective Statements	Objective Statements are considered obsolete, unless bringing the résumés to a job fair or career fair, where application letters seldom accompany a résumé. If including an Objective Statement, applicants should provide information beyond the obvious (e.g., "looking for a position in a reputable firm where I can apply my skills"). They might, for example, note type of position, field or arena, short- and long-term career path, and ways they aim to contribute to company's goals. Some applicants now favor a "Career Highlights" or "Qualification Summary" list rather than Objective Statements, but these lists are only strategic if they add to—rather than repeat—experience listed elsewhere within the résumé.	
Education	This category should be most prominent for applicants securing their first full-time position or obtaining internships while still in school; in such cases, the Education category would be most appropriate at the top of the résumé. Once applicants have held positions in the target field, industry experience becomes more prominent, allowing applicants to move the Education category to the bottom of their résumé. Regardless of its location, this category should include: • College/University, City and State • School or College within institution (e.g., College of Letters and Science, School of Public Health, Anderson School of Management) • Degree(s), linked to field of concentration, as well as program attendance or graduation date(s) For recent and soon-to-be graduates, this category might also include:	**Massachusetts Institute of Technology** *Sloan School of Management* M.B.A. in Innovation and Global Leadership, December 2016 S.B. in Management Science, May 2014 **University of San Francisco, Cupertino** *School of Nursing* Master of Nursing Science in Clinical Nurse Leader (CNL), May 2015 **University of Wisconsin–Madison** *College of Letters and Science* Bachelor of Arts in Economics with a Mathematical Emphasis, December 2016 3.896/4.0 (Overall GPA) **Universidad Complutense de Madrid** Courses in Spanish, Spanish Literature and Art History (Spring 2016) **Harold Washington, Chicago, IL** Associate in General Studies (AGS) in Information Technology, June 2016 **John Jay College of Criminal Justice, CUNY** Bachelor of Arts in Criminology, Spring 2014

Category	Guidelines and Consideration	Examples
Education (continued)	• Grade Point Average and scale (consider the pros/cons of including GPA at all, or in separating GPA into discrete "overall" and "in major" categories) • Transfer/Summer Schools • Study Abroad Programs • Coursework in programs with no degree—or no intended degree—from institution • Continuing education • Professional training and certification programs *Content Consideration:* Résumés do not focus on what could have, should have, would have, or might have been if the applicant made other choices; they focus on training and education the applicant *does* have.	**The Culinary Institute of America** St. Helena, CA *Associate Degree in Culinary Arts* (May 2014) and *Wine & Beverage Graduate Certificate* (December 2015) **Bakersfield College Bakersfield, CA** Apprenticeship Programs, Electrician and Plumbing Career Certificate, June 2012 *Courses in:* Refrigeration/AC I & II Appliances Solar Panel Installation Wiring Technologies Electricity & Energy Conservation HVAC/Plumbing
Related Coursework	This category is most appropriate for applicants securing their first full-time position or obtaining internships while still in school. After all, until people have worked in the field, their degree or course work may be the only "experience" they have to offer the industry. Once they have held positions in the target field, however, applicants should replace these entries with descriptions demonstrating their expertise in industry contexts. For applicants planning to use coursework-related categories on their résumé, they should: • Use category heading "Related Coursework," not "Relevant Coursework." The former suggests you've highlighted industry- or position-specific training; the latter suggests all but those listed are "irrelevant."	**Related Coursework** Business Communication Public Speaking I, II Entrepreneurship Ethics in Business Human Resources Management Strategic Management Production and Operations Integrated Marketing **Related Courses** Financial Accounting Ethics in the 21st Century Managerial Accounting Communication for Managers Cross-Cultural Leadership Advanced Managerial Communication Practical Leadership Mergers and Acquisitions (in progress) Technical Communication Taxes and Business Strategies (in progress)

Category	Guidelines and Consideration	Examples
Related Coursework (continued)	• Be selective. Some courses are assumed in the degree(s), so this list typically calls out upper-level electives and courses highlighting skills that set you apart from other applicants with comparable programs and degrees. • Use official course titles, rather than university course codes, numbers, and abbreviations. • Ensure course titles replicate (or correlate with) course titles that appear on transcripts—especially if transcripts may follow initial application materials. Applicants listing courses on their résumés could present coursework within the "Education" category, or make the list a stand-alone "Related Course" category.	**Western Kentucky University, Bowling Green, KY** *Bachelor of Science in Public Health*, May 2014 *Related Courses* Public Policy Implementation • Elements of Economic Analysis I • Economics for Public Policy • The Business of Non-Profits • Statistical Methods and Applications • Statistical Models and Methods • Qualitative Methods in Public Policy • Public Policy Field Research I, II **OR** **Western Kentucky University, Bowling Green, KY** *Bachelor of Science in Public Health*, May 2014 **Related Courses** Public Policy Implementation Elements of Economic Analysis I Economics for Public Policy The Business of Non-Profits Statistical Methods and Applications Statistical Models and Methods Qualitative Methods in Public Policy Public Policy Field Research I, II
Work History **or** **Experience**	The category heading "Work History" suggests paid positions, while "Experience" can include paid and non-paid positions. Whatever the title, applicants should include the following details: • Organization (full, official name, resisting acronyms upon first reference), Division, City and State • Position(s) or Title(s), which can readily show advancement within a particular organization in ways separate listings do not • Month and years of employment, being careful not to mislead or misrepresent dates of employment	WORK HISTORY **California Nature Conservatory (CNC), Chico, CA** *Human Resources Manager* (October 2013 to present) • Administer compensation, benefits and performance management systems, and safety and recreation programs • Identify staff vacancies and recruit, interview, and select applicants • Provide employees with information about policies, job duties, working conditions, wages, opportunities for promotion, and employee benefits • Analyze and modify compensation and benefits policies to establish competitive programs, ensuring compliance with legal requirements

Category	Guidelines and Consideration	Examples
Work History **or** **Experience** (continued)	• Descriptions that... ...use phrases, not complete sentences ...start with a verb ...use verb tenses to convey whether work is ongoing (present tense) or no longer being done (past tense) ...present any listed information in parallel construction ...specify what, exactly, the task entailed, rationale for doing the work, and result of efforts *Content Consideration:* Tempting as it may be to reference offers the job applicant ultimately did not accept (e.g., offers for job, promotions, projects the candidate turned down), résumés do not focus on what could have, should have, would have, or might have happened if the applicant made other choices; they focus on the positions, activities, experiences, and choices the applicant *did* pursue. As such, this section should address only the experience the applicant does, in fact, have.	PowerHub Accounting, El Sobrante, CA *Accounting Clerk II* (September 2010 to October 2013) • Keyed daily worksheets to the general ledger • Processed credit card payments and credits to generate batch deposits • Prepared requisitions for office, computer, and routine supply purchases • Filed paid and unpaid invoices and statements *Accounting Clerk I* (August 2008 to September 2010) • Reviewed and maintained division's accounting records, including those that calculated expenditures, receipts, accounts payable and receivable • Prepared requisitions for office, computer, and routine supply purchases **OR** EXPERIENCE Zinser, Meyers and Associates, Marion, IL *Writing Consultant* (August 2009 to Present). Lead workshops for all staff members of an engineering marketing firm. Supplement company-wide training with sector-specific meetings to help division employees use communication to promote sector-specific goals. Science, Technology & Policy Studies (STPS), Chicago, IL *Editorial Intern* (January 2008 to July 2009). Copyedited articles and STPS seminar papers. Input editorial changes and corrections to manuscripts. Created indicies for publications in Adobe InDesign. Prepared seminar papers for a Meyer Foundation-sponsored publication. Corresponded with authors to clarify information and editor queries. Verified editorial changes before submitting manuscripts for publication.

Category	Guidelines and Consideration	Examples
Skills	A distinct "Skills" section organizes applicant's experiences and abilities under discrete skills, ***without*** connecting those skills to specific organizations. (See examples at right; the top version incorrectly cites individual organizations in the skills section, underlined for effect; the bottom version removes these references, listing specific companies in the résumé's "Experience" section.) In addition to describing experience with various soft skills, this category might list: • Language abilities (indicate proficiency in reading, writing, and speaking) • Computer competencies (languages, software, platforms) • Research/Lab equipment Depending on the target position, applicant, experience, and so on, information that might appear in a "Skills" categories may be more appropriate to address in application letters or during interviews. *Content Consideration:* As explained in the "Experience" section, applicants may want to reference opportunities they could have pursued, but résumés focus on the opportunities the applicant did, in fact, follow. As such, this section should address only the skills the applicant has, in fact, developed.	**NOT...** SKILLS **Project Management.** Determine AlphaBean's staffing requirements. Hire, train, and supervise Peyoux, Inc. reporting staff according to company policy. Establish Xira's employee goals and objectives, and meet with staff members to discuss strategies for meeting targets. **Communication**. Develop, implement, and identify strategies in communicating for Orzo Press. Facilitate positive media, publicity and marketing campaigns, public relations programs, special events, and fundraising efforts for the City of Davis's 2013 American Cancer Association Awareness Days. Respond to inquiries from the media and arrange press conferences for Awareness Days event. Prepare web publications. **BUT...** SKILLS **Project Management.** Determine staffing requirements. Hire, train, and supervise direct reporting staff according to company policy. Establish employee goals and objectives, and meet with staff members to discuss strategies for meeting targets. **Communication.** Develop, implement, and identify strategies in communicating. Facilitate positive social media, publicity and marketing campaigns, PR programs, special events, and fundraising efforts. Respond to inquiries from the media. Arrange press conferences. Prepare web publications. EXPERIENCE • **AlphaBean**, City, State. *Title* (dates) • **Xira**, City, State. *Title* (dates) • **Peyoux, Inc.**, City, State. *Title* (dates) • **American Cancer Society Awareness Days**, City, State. *Title* (dates) • **Orzo Press**, City, State. *Title* (dates)

<table>
<tr><th>Category</th><th>Guidelines and Consideration</th><th>Examples</th></tr>
<tr><td>Skills

(continued)</td><td></td><td>ADDITIONAL "SKILLS" POSSIBLITIES (SAMPLES)
Computer Programs: ChemSketch, ChemAxon, Rasmol, Accelrys Discovery Studio Visualizer, Tarbase

Laboratory Protocols. Using, cleaning, and drying Standard-Taper glassware. Gravity Filtration. Vacuum Filtration. Extraction. Evaporation.

Languages: Cantonese (Intermediate speaking and writing), Mandarin (Beginning speaking)</td></tr>
<tr><td>Volunteer Work or Activities</td><td colspan="2">Entries for either the "Volunteer Work" or "Activities" category could be included under the larger "Experience" category since both forums offer additional training ground to develop the skills the applicant brings to a position; the position might be identified as "Volunteer" if another, formal title is unavailable. Some applicants, however, like to distinguish Experience, Volunteer, and Activities categories to suggest they have interests and talent beyond the office. Regardless of whether they are part of or distinct from entries under "Experience," these experiences should use the same formatting set-up as entries in the "Experience" category (i.e., entries should include full names of the organization, divisions, city, state, title/position, and so on).

When deciding how or if to include these experiences on a résumé, applicants should consider ways this information might represent "Hot Topics," details that may reveal the applicant's values, identity, biases… in ways that may not be valued by prospective employers. Hot topics include affiliations to particular religions, political parties, races, social fraternities/sororities, socio-economic status, sexual orientation, and so on. This note is neither an endorsement for nor admonition against including these items on a résumé; rather, it's a reminder that the job application process is inherently biased as people look for applicants "like them." Therefore, details in this area can help employers make such assessments in ways applicants do—or don't—intend.</td></tr>
<tr><td>Honors and Awards</td><td>This category should include the Sponsor, Official Award Name, Your Title (e.g., Recipient, Finalist, Nominee, Honoree), Month/Term, Year(s), and so forth, using the same formatting hierarchies as entries in other categories.</td><td>Baker University Dean's List (Fall 2009, Spring 2011)

Samuel R. Hunting Annual Public Service Award, Nominee (2008–2010, 2012)

Heartland Tribune's University Scholar-Athlete of the Year, Recipient (2014)

The Society of Women Engineers' Suzanne Jenniches Upward Mobility Award, Recipient (2015)

The Rotary Foundation Distinguished Service Award, Recipient (2012)</td></tr>
</table>

Category	Guidelines and Consideration	Examples
Languages	This category can represent cultural linguistics, as well as scripting/programming languages for computers. For clarification, applicants may need to indicate degree of fluency in specific literacy practices, platforms, and so on. Depending on space constraints and relevance to the target job position, this information could be presented more appropriately in the application letter or during an interview, if anywhere.	SKILLS: *Languages*: Spanish (advanced reading, wrinting, and speaking), German (conversational), French (native fluency) *Computer Languages:* HTML, Java, Javascript, Lua, COBOL, C, C++, Erlang, PHP, Perl, TCL, and Unix/Linux
Certifications	This category can be of value if proficiency in a particular field or profession is indicated or supplemented by certificates (e.g., real estate, interior design, travel agent). Certification can be listed near or even within the "Education" category, or in a separate category in the résumé.	**Chartered Financial Analyst (CFA)**, August 2015 **Certified Financial Planner (CFP)**, November 2016 **Certified Chiropractic Sports Physician (CCSP)**, May 2012 **International Chiropractic Sport Science Diplomate (ICSSD)**, May 2009
Professional Affiliations and Memberships	Like certifications, a category for professional affiliations and membership can be of value if proficiency in the target field or profession is indicated or supplemented by sustained engagement with other experts. This information can be listed near or even within the "Education" category, or in a separate category in the résumé. Regardless of this information's location, applicants should use a set up comparable to "Experience" entries, (i.e., include the full, official name of organization; branch or chapter; position or title in relationship to the organization, if any; dates of affiliation).	**American Society of Interior Designer (ASIDs)**, *Allied Member* (2012 to present) **American Academy of Ophthalmology**, *Member* (2010 to present) **Council of Real Estate Brokerage Managers** (CRB), *Member* (2004–2012) **Industrial Designers Society of America** (IDSA), San Francisco Chapter, *Active Member* (2013 to present) **International Association of Business Communication (IABC), University of Illinois at Urbana–Champaign**, *Student Affiliate* (Fall 2015 to present) **American Hotel and Lodging Association, UC Berkeley**, Delta Chapter, *Member* (Fall 2010 to Spring 2013)
Hobbies and Interests	This category can offer insight into the applicant, providing they are hobbies and interests that the applicant actually does or participates in on a regular basis. Applicants should, however, be cautious about listing entries that can seem philosophically or socially at odds with the target position, its demands, and its values.	

Category	Guidelines and Consideration	Examples
References	Employers assume applicants can secure and provide references. Therefore, rather than devote a line on the résumé to write what's taken for granted (e.g., "References Available Upon Request"), applicants might list the names, titles, and contact details of their professional references on a separate page—or even in a distinct document—and have it ready at an interview, in case the hiring manager asks for references at that time.	
Salary History **or** **Target Salary**	Omit this category, even when requested. Noting a salary history or target salary can make any salary negotiations harder, or even impossible. Consider, for example, that applicants might unknowingly lowball themselves with a lower-than-typical salary range. Or, if the numbers are higher than the employer is willing to go, applicants can suggest they are unwilling to take a lower salary for the right configuration of other elements. To keep the conversations open, applicants should omit salary information—on both the résumé and in the application letter—and, instead, save the discussion for when there's an actual offer on the table and for when the applicant knows (or can further discuss) what, exactly, the work entails in the context(s) it needs to be done.	

In reviewing this chart, you may find information that suits your immediate purposes, and you may wonder about other information or categories. Assuming you can account for your time in ways that minimize gaps in your employment history, you may be able to select details that best reflect *your* candidacy for a position. Along the way, if you find that some of this information does not work on the résumé itself—either because of space constraints or questions of audience—it may be possible to include it in the application letter or address it during an interview.

Exercise: Résumé Content Review

For this exercise, you need a hard copy of your résumé. Considering the information that would appeal most to hiring managers in your target field, use the "Conventional Résumé Categories" chart on the previous pages to indentify information your résumé:

- *should* keep or include,
- *should not* keep or include, and
- *might* keep or include, depending on your target field or industry, or other circumstances you could justify

As you review your résumé, consider how each category's Guidelines and Considerations might help you recognize information to elaborate upon, clarify, or tighten in your résumé.

Secret 8: Job responsibilities matter less than verifiable performance.

Trying to explain the work they have done for an organization, many applicants lift phrases from their job description. Although job descriptions may offer a starting point for résumé entries, duties and responsibilities say little about an employee's contribution to the company and, therefore, offer minimal information for hiring managers looking for top performers. Consider, for example, the following entries, taken from résumés in various industries:

> Duties included managing the work flow, troubleshooting, and monitoring quality assurance.
>
> Hired to solve and fix any production line problems with the help of service engineers.
>
> Responsible for managing day-to-day coverage of news under the instructions of the chief editor.
>
> Responsibilities included entering data into LIMS system.
>
> Duties included providing reference services to faculty and students.
>
> Responsible for selecting new and original manuscripts.
>
> Duties included receiving, preparing, and processing laboratory specimens received from patients.

Granted, hiring managers in the industry may be able to decipher the value of some of the work depicted by these statements, but focusing descriptions around duties and responsibilities never clarifies whether the person actually engaged in or completed these tasks—the descriptors simply indicate what the employee was *supposed* to do. Thus, one of the first and easiest steps for ensuring performance-oriented descriptors is to remove the "responsibilities include...," "responsible for...," "duties include...," and "hired to..." references, and start on the verb:

> **Manage** the work flow, **troubleshoot**, and **monitor** quality assurance.
>
> **Solve** and **fix** any production line problems with the help of service engineers.
>
> **Manage** day-to-day coverage of news under the instructions of the chief editor.
>
> **Enter** data into LIMS system.
>
> **Provide** reference services to faculty and students.
>
> **Select** new and original manuscripts.
>
> **Receive**, **prepare**, and **process** laboratory specimens received from patients.

Starting on the verb instantly transforms the descriptions to focus on employee actions, rather than leave the employee's performance in question. This change also makes it easier to adjust verb tenses to clarify whether the individual is still doing the work.

The following entries, for example, use the present tense, which suggests the person is still doing these tasks:

> Manage the work flow, troubleshoot, and monitor quality assurance.
>
> Solve and fix any production line problems with the help of service engineers.
>
> Manage day-to-day coverage of news under the instructions of the chief editor.
>
> Enter data into LIMS system.
>
> Provide reference services to faculty and students.

> Select new and original manuscripts.
>
> Receive, prepare, and process laboratory specimens received from patients.

If, however, the individual is no longer doing this work—either because the person has moved on to other responsibilities, into a different position, or even to another company—the past tense clarifies that the individual has done the work, but is no longer engaged in these efforts:

> Manage**d** the work flow, trouble**shot**, and monitor**ed** quality assurance.
>
> Solve**d** and fix**ed** any production line problems with the help of service engineers.
>
> Manage**d** day-to-day coverage of news under the instructions of the chief editor.
>
> Enter**ed** data into LIMS system.
>
> Provide**d** reference services to faculty and students.
>
> Select**ed** new and original manuscripts.
>
> Receive**d**, prepare**d**, and processe**d** laboratory specimens received from patients.

Removing the phrase "responsible for" or "duties include" can be sufficient. Sometimes, however, descriptions need more editing to distinguish job-related tasks from, say, job titles or employment forums, as the following entry demonstrates:

> Duties include a combination of the following: eligibility verification, intake, interviewing, referrals to supportive services, career coaching, employer services, social service facilitation, job search and orientation/ classroom instruction, and regular follow-up in evaluating and executing each client's individual employment plan.

This job description may identify some of the tasks an employee has been asked to perform, but simply transcribing this information into a résumé can make it harder for prospective employers to distinguish what, in fact, has been done, for whom, in what context, and with what results. Equally problematic is that eliminating the phrase "duties include…" is not enough. To use details from this and comparable job descriptions, an applicant would need to distinguish tasks from contexts; add or modify verbs for consistency; and reorder or, perhaps, regroup related or overlapping actions.

The next secret will make such work easier but, to prepare for that work, it's time to make sure your own résumé descriptions focus on actions you have performed.

Exercise: Tightening Résumé Descriptors

This editing exercise is a starting point for tightening your résumé descriptions, setting you up for later exercises.

Step 1. Print out a copy of your résumé.

Step 2. Highlight the phrases "responsibilities include…," "duties include…," "responsible for…," and comparable references.

Step 3. Identify the *main* verb(s) in each descriptor; ultimately, these verbs will *start* the description.

Step 4. Write verb(s) in present tense if you are still doing this work; change verb(s) to past tense if you are no longer doing this work.

Step 5. Start each description in your résumé—both those you edited for this exercise, as well as those you did not—on the *verb.* (You, the applicant, are the presumed grammatical subject for every entry in your résumé, so you can save space, omit references to yourself, and start with the action.)

The editorial changes in this exercise may seem superficial, but they shift what you offer prospective employers in critical ways. First, they shift the focus from lists of abstract duties and responsibilities to concrete actions you have performed. Second, they tighten the overall presentation of information, freeing up valuable real estate on the résumé that you can use to offer more tangible explanations of what you did, as we'll discuss in the next secret.

Secret 9: Too much hype and too little substance make applicants seem insecure, or even desperate.

Many job applicants work to convince prospective employers that they're not just qualified for a position, but that they're the *most* qualified, often engaging in linguistic gymnastics to express superlative qualifications to the hiring manager. In such cases, applicants are never average; they are *excellent*, *outstanding*, *exceptional*. And their skill sets are never just sufficient; they are *wide-ranging*, *comprehensive*, *superb*, *extraordinary*.

Stanley J. Randall, former vice-president of the Canadian Manufacturer's Association and chairman of the Ontario Economic Council, once observed that "the closest to perfection a person ever comes is when filling out a job application," and the following descriptors—representative excerpts from "Summary of Qualifications" sections of résumés in various industries—echo Randall's observation:

> Comprehensive knowledge of accounting, tax preparation and financial planning.
>
> Thorough understanding of human psychology and behavior.
>
> Proven client relationship builder with unsurpassed sales and negotiation skills.
>
> Exemplary leadership skills, able to inspire and guide others on a range of assignments in various contexts.
>
> Excellent planning, organizational, and management skills.
>
> Optimal problem solver that excels in meeting the highest performance standards.
>
> Highly motivated, resourceful, and innovative team player.

Exceptional communication abilities, both written and verbal.

Tremendous knowledge of programming languages like C, C++, VB, JAVA, .NET etc..

Extensive knowledge of building and sensitizing comprehensive financial models, performing far-reaching financial and business due diligence, and creating detailed internal credit documents.

Intimate familiarity with curriculum and administrative procedures at all educational levels.

Exceptional work ethics with a significant ability to solve work-related problems immediately.

Excellent computer knowledge, development of promotional materials, database entry and management, and correspondence.

Emotionally stable, able to handle extremely stressful situations.

Enthusiastic self-starter, who excels in offering excellent customer service.

Possess excellent customer/goal-orientation interpersonal, communication, and PC skills.

As applicants pull out their thesaurus or scour the internet for adjectives that suggest they're matchless in every qualification, application materials increasingly portray supernatural individuals who are able to process data and solve complex problems faster than a speeding bullet, bend competitors' minds with their will, and leap industry hurdles in a single bound. Unfortunately, unless you're planning to show up to an interview wearing a cape, there are problems with this approach to the job search.

Describing every skill and ability with superlatives and other hyperbolic language, for example, can suggest you don't have credible standards or reference points of evaluation; consequently, when everything is depicted as amazing, extraordinary, stellar, top-notch, and so on, hiring mangers become skeptical of the most basic assertions. Moreover, by relying on "powerful language" to sell your skills rather than tangible evidence, you run the risk of appearing arrogant and cocky, rather than competent. There is, however, a way you can present your capabilities accurately, authentically, and competitively, once you understand the secret concerning relative terms.

This secret affects résumés and application letters, but it does so in different ways. Therefore, applying this secret in either forum hinges on your ability to recognize and replace relative terms, which dominate the application materials circulating in today's market.

Consider some of the earlier "Summary of Qualification" entries, each of which contains one or more relative terms:

> **Comprehensive** knowledge of accounting, tax preparation and financial planning
>
> **Thorough** understanding of human psychology and behavior
>
> **Proven** client relationship builder with **unsurpassed** sales and negotiation skills
>
> **Exemplary** leadership skills, able to inspire and guide others on a **range of assignments** in **various** contexts
>
> **Excellent** planning, organizational and management skills
>
> **Optimal** problem solver that excels in meeting **the highest performance standards**
>
> **Highly motivated**, **resourceful**, and **innovative** team player
>
> **Exceptional** communication abilities, both written and verbal

Relative terms are words—typically adjectives, but also concepts—that assume *identical* points of reference for defining, gauging, and understanding what *comprehensive*, *thorough*, *proven*, *unsurpassed*, and so on means in a particular context. Applicants may know what *they* mean when they use these words, and hiring managers may know what *they* mean when they see or hear these words, but whether applicants and hiring managers mean *exactly* the same thing is unclear, and unlikely.

When people do not share *identical* points of reference, relative terms become "relative" to each participant's individual point of reference. Consider gruff service representatives who describe themselves as "customer-oriented," or "supportive" managers that bark orders to their subordinates, or "team players" who are absent from most project discussions. These different interpretations and, by extension, different understandings of terms and phrases, inevitably result in miscommunication—especially in written communication.

Oral communication has the advantage of stress, tone, pitch, rhythm, pace and so on to help convey meaning. Face-to-face communication has the added benefits of facial expressions and body language. Written communication, however, relies on what's printed on the page or what appears on the screen, and we cannot always guarantee readers will see, hear, or interpret words as we intend.

Take, for example, the sentence "That was really interesting." Speaking to an audience, we could alter our meaning simply by emphasizing particular words. To demonstrate, read the following sentences aloud, stressing the word that's italicized:

> *That* was really interesting.
>
> That *was* really interesting.
>
> That was *really* interesting.
>
> That was really *interesting*.

By simply emphasizing different words in our speech, we can encourage an audience toward surprise, agreement, enthusiasm, or cynicism. Yet, written communication is different. We cannot write something like the following and retain our professionalism:

> That was **really** INTERESTING!! ☺☺

We can, however, accurately convey our meaning by giving indisputable facts. In other words, we need to identify and replace the relative terms.

Before discussing how you can make this shift in your application materials, we'll start with non-job related sentences to show how to replace relative terms with details that others can understand—regardless of their context, background, and biases.

> **Original:**
> This building is tall.

In this example, the adjective "tall" is the relative term. What "tall" means depends on a person's experiences and frames of reference for architectural structures. A resident of New York City, for instance, will define a "tall" building differently than a resident of earthquake-prone San Francisco, or a resident of an Iowa farming community. Therefore, if we want each of these individuals—and countless others—to understand exactly what *we* mean by "tall," we must provide tangible, uncontested details that others can use, test, evaluate, research, and so on. So, how do we identify the details we should offer?

One strategy is the "*X* was so *Y*" trope comedians would use to encourage audiences to respond, "How *Y* is it?" or "How *Y* was it?" In the case of our example, "The building is tall…" would prompt the response, "How tall is it?" Comedians might offer a punch line, but we would offer details to answer the audience's question.

> **Revisions:**
> The building is 75 stories.
> The building is 750–1050 feet high. (assuming 10–14 feet per floor).

Such information needs no additional commentary or qualifiers to help readers interpret what we mean (e.g., "The building is really tall—75 stories!"). The details we offer should speak for themselves, allowing readers to understand the structure is tall, massive, conventional, or any other adjective *they* might provide on their own, based on the details we offer, and those we don't. Here's another example.

> **Original:**
> We are looking for a quick turn-around on the Olivier project.

The audience call-back might be, "How quick is 'quick'?" And while it may be tempting to offer a response like, "As soon as possible" or "ASAP," such responses are relative, providing a time-frame that varies from person to person. For some, "as soon as possible" may represent by the end of the day; for others, it may be next week or even next month, increasing the possibilities for miscommunication.

If the "*X* was so *Y*" trope cannot generate the details an audience might want or need to understand information as we intend, we might turn to the conventional "Five Ws" that guide journalists (Who? What? Where? When? Why?), perhaps adding the questions "How?" and "So what?" to the list. With this strategy, the statement "We are looking for a quick turn-around on the Olivier project" might prompt a revision that answers the following questions: "*Who* needs the project?" "By *when*?" "*Why*?" "*Where* do I submit it?" and "*How* do I submit it?"

> **Revision:**
> To ensure the department meets this year's budget request submission deadline of May 1, 20XX, please email the Olivier project to <jdoe@anyserver.com> by 5pm, Friday, April 23.

One final example addresses adverbs, because they, too, appear in job application materials.

> **Original:**
> The Canon XE-3 copy machine can print documents really fast.

If we were to use the "*X* was so *Y*" trope "How fast does it print?" readers might say the answer is already in the original: *really* fast. But the adverb "really"—and all of its synonyms, including *very*, *incredibly*, *enormously*, and *truly*—are relative, since not everyone holds the same measures of gradation.

All Olympic sprinters, for example, are "really fast," especially when compared to non-competitive runners. Still, as these athletes would confirm, 1/100th of a second can, in fact, distinguish how fast is "fast." Therefore, providing indisputable facts gives readers information they can use to make the decisions they may want and need to make.

> **Revision:**
> The Canon XE-3 copy machine can print 30 pages per minute in black and white, and 20 pages per minute in color.

Although some people might argue that details strip away the power and the beauty of adjectives, writing is about communication—conveying information and ideas others can use, often in the writer's absence. And this objective becomes more evident in job application materials, which hiring managers must use to determine if an applicant can actually do the work required by the position, or if that person is simply making heroic claims.

Consider once again the "Summary of Qualification" entries with one or more relative terms:

> **Comprehensive** knowledge of accounting, tax preparation and financial planning
>
> **Thorough** understanding of human psychology and behavior
>
> **Proven** client relationship builder with **unsurpassed** sales and negotiation skills
>
> **Exemplary** leadership skills, able to inspire and guide others on a **range of assignments** in **various** contexts

Running through the "*X* was so *Y*" trope, or the reporter's "Five Ws," and the questions "How?" and "So What?," we can understand the concerns hiring managers may have about the applicant's professed expertise. "Comprehensive" according to what standards? "Thorough" by whose definition? "Unsurpassed" in what forum? What constitutes a "range of assignments" and how "varied" are the contexts? Such questions, left unanswered, make it harder for hiring managers to gauge what an applicant has done and, more importantly, what the applicant can do in the available position—especially since claiming competency doesn't make it so.

Recognizing that hiring managers need information to understand an applicant's credentials, we now turn to examine how to address relative terms in application materials. Take, for example, the following résumé entry:

> **Original:**
> Provide valuable reference services to faculty and students.

Certainly a company's name or a job title might help hiring managers infer what type of reference services the applicant offers, but few hiring managers will take the time to guess all that this work may involve. By unpacking the relative terms and clarifying *what* they did, *when* they did it, *how* they did it, *for whom* they did, and the *results* of those efforts, applicants can minimize misunderstanding and shape how they position themselves on the market.

Notice, for example, how the following, possible revisions create different expectation for what hiring managers might see in an applicant:

> **Revision 1:**
> Use Dynic, Dynix Elite, OPAC, and NOTIS library systems to help faculty members locate, order and track scholarly books and journals from within the university's 10-campus, inter-library loan system.
>
> **Revision 2:**
> Research and maintain databank of medical professionals, emergency care centers, pharmacies, laboratory testing sites, and other health facilities within the state to address patient needs that are not available on campus, or covered by university health insurance plans. Create, update, and circulate posters, fliers, and brochures with information each semester for distribution to 35,500 campus community members.
>
> **Revision 3:**
> Provide supplementary legal information and referrals to students, faculty and staff members in the areas of consumer protection, civil actions, adoption and family law, bankruptcy, tenancy issues, personal injury and estate planning.

This secret gets more attention than most because it addresses one of the most critical elements of application documents in general, and résumés in particular: describing your training, experiences and abilities in ways that help others know what you have done and how. Consequently, learning and applying this secret alone would distinguish your résumé from countless others presently circulating.

Revising and generating descriptions to offer tangible, uncontested details takes time. After all, moving beyond superficial assertions of proficiency requires matter-of-fact descriptions of what we have done so that others know what it took to do that work in the contexts, in the ways, and with the resources we had at our disposal. The following content and set-up can help generate such information:

For Tasks You *Are Still Doing...*

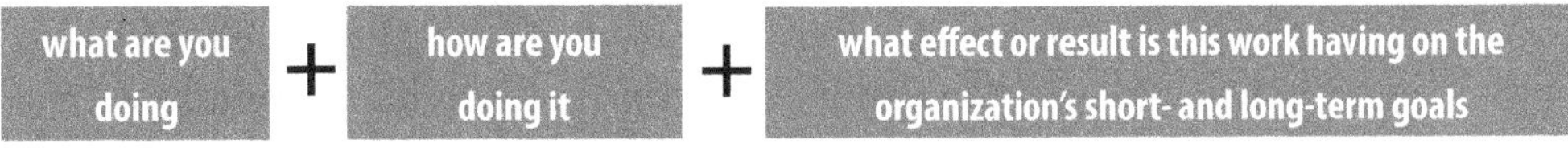
what are you doing
+
how are you doing it
+
what effect or result is this work having on the organization's short- and long-term goals

For Tasks You *Have Done...*

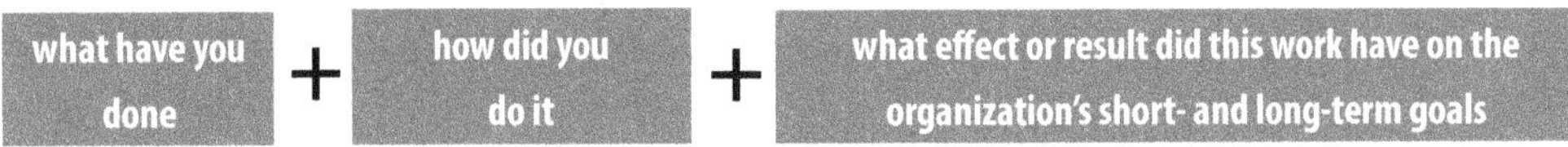
what have you done
+
how did you do it
+
what effect or result did this work have on the organization's short- and long-term goals

The following résumé descriptions adopt this structure, using both present tense and past tense to indicate on-going and former work, respectively:

> Arrange and facilitate monthly conference calls with 10–15 division managers and participate in *ad hoc* employee discussions to generate ideas and to discuss strategies for meeting quarterly sales targets.
>
> Work with sales team managers to design opt-in training workshops series to help employees who volunteer to participate learn about, practice, and improve cold-calling techniques, resulting in maximum capacity attendance for each session and an 8% increase in company's sales within six months.
>
> Use Dealogic, Bloomberg, Factiva, FactSet, and Thompson One Banker to prepare leveraged buyouts, mergers & acquisitions, and valuation models based on product-appropriate valuation methodologies, helping to drive over $500 million in revenues.
>
> Develop and maintain client relationships prior to and through deal execution by organizing, attending, and occasionally hosting sponsor meetings and by serving as the primary contact person during deal opportunity discussions.
>
> Identified company strengths and areas for improvement by tracking and analyzing 24 months of customer surveys, and used resulting data to create a training manual that has been implemented in employee orientations in eight regional stores, ensuring greater consistency in customer service.

> Used Integrated Library Systems (ILS) databases to cross-check and, when necessary, research bibliography and citation information for completion and accuracy before reformatting articles to comply with the master style guide for inclusion in division's annual proceedings.
>
> Used Adobe Photoshop CS6 and InDesign to design, and format newsletter distributed electronically each month to over 6,000 subscribers of *Nutrition Now Journal.*

Again, generating relative term-free descriptions takes time but, with practice, you will become more familiar with the type of information to include in descriptions, changing the ways you begin to talk about and describe the work you do to others.

As importantly, you will have and retain greater control over how hiring managers understand your experience; specifically, they will not need to guess, or infer, what you *may* be able to do, because you have explicitly identified what you *can* do. The following exercise moves you forward in this endeavor.

Exercise: Résumé Show or Tell?

This activity focuses on conveying what you do—or what you have done—to those who may not have first-hand knowledge of the work you have performed. For this exercise, you will need a hard copy of your résumé. For additional room to make comments and edits, you might consider double spacing your résumé before printing it.

Step 1. Moving through each résumé category and description, highlight the relative terms (adjectives, adverbs, concepts) that assume identical points of reference.

Step 2. Ask yourself, "What information do readers need to understand what I did, as I did it, in the forum(s) in which I did it?" for each element you highlighted. To generate information that might appear in a revised description, use the "*X* was so *Y*" trope, and provide details to clarify "How *Y* was it?" Or, use conventional reporter questions (Who? What? Where? When? Why? How?), and add "So what?" to identify short- and long-term effects.

Step 3. Answer each question with concrete, tangible details (e.g., dollar figures, percentages, numbers, ranges, software programs, industry protocols, actions, sequence of actions), one description at a time.

Step 4. Revise each highlighted résumé entry to incorporate your answers into the descriptions.

In moving through these steps, the descriptions and, by extension, your résumé will become longer, but you should resist the urge to censor yourself at this stage. For now, focus on providing the most complete and accurate information to help readers understand what each job or task has entailed as *you* performed it.

Once you have clarified what you have done, you will be able to identify which information to keep; which to combine and condense; which to reserve for particular audiences, perhaps in a targeted résumé; and, which might be more effective in another context, say in an application letter or interview.

Secret 10: Applicants should use the type of résumé that emphasizes the abilities they have for the position they seek.

Some industries adopt a "one-size-fits-all" model, suggesting a single product or service can satisfy a range of needs and interests, but this model seldom works in a job search. Training and expertise can be vastly different, yet job applicants frequently adopt the single-model mentality when they assume a chronological résumé is the best—or only—option to convey their experience.

Certainly many *employers* may prefer chronological résumés, because they can quickly see where, when, and how applicants have spent time in a given field, but chronological résumés aren't effective or appropriate for every job applicant. Therefore, understanding the types of résumés can help you project your experiences and abilities in the best possible light.

The following pages give an overview of résumé formats on the market.

Reverse Chronological Résumés

A (reverse) chronological résumé is the most commonly used and, perhaps, the most familiar type of résumé, emphasizing an applicant's employment history. Using reverse chronological order (i.e., starting each category with the most current position or experience and moving back in time to the least current positions and experiences), chronological résumés identify the organization the applicant has worked with, the position(s) held, and work the applicant did for each.

Chronological résumés are appropriate for applicants who have consistent employment, ideally in a single industry. Chronological résumés help applicants highlight their longevity within the larger field or within a particular company, their sequential advancement, and their increase in responsibilities.

Jurrich "Jake" Snyder
123 Main Street, El Cerrito, CA 94530
510-555-1212
jsnyder@anyserver.com

Education

College/University , City, State
College or School
Degree in Major, with a concentration in Minor, Month Year

Experience

Company/Organization's Name, City, State
Title/Position (Month Year–Month Year). Lorem ipsum dolor sit amet, consectetuer adipiscing elit, sed diam nonummy nibh euismod tincidunt ut laoreet dolore magna aliquam erat volutpat. Ut wisi enim ad minim veniam, quis nostrud exerci tation ullamcorper suscipit lobortis nisl ut aliquip ex ea commodo consequat. Lorem ipsum dolor sit amet. Ut wisi enim ad minim veniam, quis nostrud exerci tation ullamcorper suscipit lobortis nisl ut aliquip ex ea commodo consequat.

Company/Organization's Name, City, State
Title/Position (Month Year–Month Year). Duis autem vel eum iriure dolor in hendrerit in vulputate velit esse molestie consequat, vel illum dolore eu feugiat nulla facilisis at vero eros et accumsan et iusto odio dignissim qui blandit. Consectetuer adipiscing elit, sed diam nonummy nibh euismod tincidunt ut laoreet dolore magna aliquam erat volutpat. Ut wisi enim ad minim veniam, quis nostrud exerci tation ullamcorper suscipit lobortis nisl ut aliquip ex ea commodo consequat. Duis autem vel eum iriure dolor in hendrerit.

Title/Position (Month Year–Month Year). Lorem ipsum dolor sit amet, consectetuer adipiscing elit, sed diam nonummy nibh euismod tincidunt ut laoreet dolore magna aliquam erat volutpat. vero eros et accumsan et iusto odio dignissim qui blandit praesent luptatum zzril delenit augue duis dolore te feugait nulla facilisi. Lorem ipsum dolor sit amet, consectetuer adipiscing elit, sed diam nonummy nibh euismod tincidunt ut laoreet dolore magna aliquam erat volutpat consectetuer adipiscing elit. Sed diam nonummy nibh euismod tincidunt ut laoreet dolore magna aliquam erat volutpat.

Company/Organization's Name, City, State
Title/Position (Month Year–Month Year). Iriure dolor in hendrerit in vulputate velit esse molestie consequat, vel illum dolore eu feugiat nulla facilisis at vero eros et accumsan et iusto odio dignissim qui blandit praesent luptatum zzril delenit augue duis dolore te feugait nulla facilisi. Lorem ipsum dolor sit amet, consectetuer adipiscing elit.

Company/Organization's Name, City, State
Title/Position (Month Year–Month Year). Tincidunt ut laoreet dolore magna aliquam erat volutpat. Ut wisi enim ad minim veniam, quis nostrud exerci tation ullamcorper suscipit lobortis nisl ut aliquip ex ea commodo consequat.

Activities

Company/Organization's Name, City, State
Title/Position (Month Year–Month Year). Lorem ipsum dolor sit amet, consectetuer adipiscing elit, sed diam nonummy nibh euismod tincidunt ut laoreet dolore magna aliquam erat volutpat. Ut wisi enim ad minim. Vel illum dolore eu feugiat nulla facilisis at vero eros et accumsan et iusto odio dignissim qui blandit praesent luptatum zzril delenit augue duis dolore te feugait nulla facilisi.

Company/Organization's Name, City, State
Title/Position (Month Year–Month Year). Lorem ipsum dolor sit amet, consectetuer adipiscing elit, sed diam Duis autem vel eum iriure dolor in hendrerit in vulputate velit esse molestie consequat, vel illum dolore.

Chronological Résumé Sample

Functional Résumés

A functional résumé (also known as a "skills-based résumé") focuses on professional expertise and competencies the applicant has acquired and, ideally, applied in various contexts—regardless of whether the applicant has received financial compensation for that work. Focusing on what the applicant can do, rather than where the applicant did it, the functional résumé emphasizes skills of value in an industry.

Functional résumés are appropriate for applicants who may have little or no formal experience in the profession itself. They are also effective for people entering or transferring into a field, as well as for applicants who may have gaps in their employment history. Increasingly, functional résumés are finding favor with over-qualified applicants, since this type of résumé downplays specific organizations and titles/positions and, instead, promotes skills and accomplishments related to the position of interest.

Mary P. Silver
4567 Main Street, El Cerrito, CA 94530 | 510-555-1212 | mpsilver@anyserver.com

Education
College/University , City, State
College or School
Degree in Major, with a concentration in Minor

Skills
Finance/Accounting
Lorem ipsum dolor sit amet, consectetuer adipiscing elit, sed diam nonummy nibh euismod tincidunt ut laoreet dolore magna aliquam erat volutpat. Ut wisi enim ad minim veniam, quis nostrud exerci tation ullamcorper suscipit lobortis nisl ut aliquip ex ea commodo consequat. Lorem ipsum dolor sit amet. Ut wisi enim ad minim veniam, quis nostrud exerci tation ullamcorper suscipit lobortis nisl ut aliquip ex ea commodo consequat.

Communication
Duis autem vel eum iriure dolor in hendrerit in vulputate velit esse molestie consequat, vel illum dolore eu feugiat nulla facilisis at vero eros et accumsan et iusto odio dignissim qui blandit. Ut wisi enim ad minim. Vel illum dolore eu feugiat nulla facilisis at vero eros et accumsan et iusto odio dignissim qui blandit praesent luptatum zzril delenit augue duis dolore tegna aliquam erat volutpat. Ut wisi enim ad minim veniam, quis nostrud exerci tation ullamcorper suscipit lobortis nisl ut aliquip ex ea commodo consequat. Duis autem vel eum iriure dolor in hendrerit.

Marketing
Consectetuer adipiscing elit, sed diam nonummy nibh euismod tincidunt ut laoreet dolore magna aliquam erat volutpat. vero eros et accumsan et iusto odio dignissim qui blandit praesent luptatum zzril delenit augue duis dolore te feugait nulla facilisi. Lorem ipsum dolor sit amet, consectetuer adipiscing elit, sed diam nonummy nibh euismod tincidunt ut laoreet dolore magna aliquam erat volutpat consectetuer adipiscing elit. Lorem ipsum dolor sit amet, consectetuer nibh euismod tincidunt ut laoreet dolore magna aliquam erat volutpat. Ut wisi enim ad minim. Reros et accumsan et iusto odio dignissim qui blandit praesent luptatum zzril delenit augue duis dolore te feugait nulla facilisi. Sed diam nonummy nibh euismod tincidunt ut laoreet dolore magna aliquam erat volutpat.

Research
Iriure dolor in hendrerit in vulputate velit esse molestie consequat, vel illum dolore eu feugiat nulla facilisis at vero eros et accumsan et iusto odio dignissim qui blandit praesent luptatum zzril delenit augue duis dolore te feugait nulla facilisi. Lorem ipsum dolor sit amet, consectetuer adipiscing elit.

Computers
Tincidunt ut laoreet dolore magna aliquam erat volutpat. Ut wisi enim ad minim veniam, quis nostrud exerci tation ullamcorper suscipit lobortis nisl ut aliquip ex ea commodo consequat. Lorem ipsum dolor sit amet, consectetuer adipiscing elit, sed diam Duis autem vel eum iriure dolor in hendrerit in vulputate velit esse molestie consequat, vel illum dolore.

Experience
Company/Organization's Name, City, State. *Title/Position* (Month Year–Month Year).
Company/Organization's Name, City, State. *Title/Position* (Month Year–Month Year).
Company/Organization's Name, City, State. *Title/Position* (Month Year–Month Year).

Interests Ut wisi enim ad minim. Vel illum dolore eu feugiat nulla. Facilisis at vero eros et accumsan. Iusto odio.

Functional Résumé Sample

Combination Résumés

A combination résumé blends elements of the chronological and functional résumés, letting applicants list positions they've held *and* include a separate section for job-related skills applicants acquired beyond those positions.

Combination résumés are appropriate for people who have conventional workplace experience and complementary skills that organizations in the applicant's target field use or otherwise value. Combination résumés can also help applicants whose conventional job titles and responsibilities neither suggest nor highlight the applicant's proficiency in other areas.

Targeted Résumés

Presenting information that may appear in a chronological, functional, or combination résumé, the targeted résumé is customized to address the needs and interests of a particular position in a specific organization. For example,

Anna-Maria B. Ross
9890 Elm Street, El Cerrito, CA 94530 | 510-555-1212 | ambross@anyserver.com

Education

College/University , City, State
College or School
Degree in Major, Month Year

Experience

Company/Organization's Name, City, State
Title/Position (Month Year–Month Year). Ut wisi enim ad minim veniam, quis nostrud exerci tation ullamcorper suscipit lobortis nisl ut aliquip ex ea commodo consequat. Duis autem vel eum iriure dolor in hendrerit. Lorem ipsum dolor sit amet.

Company/Organization's Name, City, State
Title/Position (Month Year–Month Year). Duis autem vel eum iriure dolor in hendrerit in vulputate velit esse molestie consequat, vel illum dolore eu feugiat nulla facilisis at vero eros et accumsan et iusto odio dignissim qui blandit. Lorem ipsum dolor sit amet, consectetuer adipiscing elit, sed diam nonummy nibh euismod tincidunt ut laoreet dolore magna aliquam erat volutpat. Ut wisi enim ad minim veniam, quis nostrud exerci tation ullamcorper suscipit lobortis nisl ut aliquip ex ea commodo consequat. Consectetuer adipiscing elit, sed diam nonummy nibh euismod tincidunt ut laoreet dolore magna aliquam erat volutpat. Tation ullamcorper suscipit lobortis nisl ut aliquip ex ea commodo consequat.

Title/Position (Month Year–Month Year). Lorem ipsum dolor sit amet, consectetuer adipiscing elit, sed diam nonummy nibh euismod tincidunt ut laoreet dolore magna aliquam erat volutpat. Sed diam nonummy nibh euismod tincidunt ut laoreet dolore magna aliquam erat volutpat consectetuer adipiscing elit. Laoreet dolore magna aliquam erat volutpat.

Skills

Strategic Planning
Euismod tincidunt ut laoreet dolore magna aliquam erat volutpat. vero eros et accumsan et iusto odio dignissim qui blandit praesent luptatum zzril delenit augue duis dolore te feugait nulla facilisi. Nonummy nibh euismod tincidunt ut laoreet dolore magna aliquam erat volutpat consectetuer adipiscing elit. Sed diam nonummy nibh euismod tincidunt ut laoreet dolore magna aliquam erat volutpat. Tincidunt ut laoreet dolore magna aliquam erat volutpat. Ut wisi enim ad minim veniam, quis nostrud exerci tation ullamcorper suscipit lobortis nisl ut aliquip ex ea commodo consequat. Lorem ipsum dolor sit amet, consectetuer adipiscing elit, sed diam.

Managerial
Duis autem vel eum iriure dolor in hendrerit in vulputate velit esse molestie consequat, vel illum dolore eu feugiat nulla facilisis at vero eros et accumsan et iusto odio dignissim qui blandit. Ut wisi enim ad minim. Vel illum dolore eu feugiat nulla facilisis at vero eros et accumsan et iusto odio dignissim qui blandit praesent luptatum zzril delenit augue duis dolore tegna aliquam erat volutpat. Ad minim veniam quis nostrud exerci tation ullamcorper. Duis autem vel eum iriure dolor in hendrerit.

Research
Nibh euismod tincidunt ut laoreet dolore magna aliquam erat volutpat. Ut wisi enim ad minim veniam, quis nostrud exerci tation ullamcorper suscipit lobortis nisl ut aliquip ex ea commodo consequat. Lorem ipsum dolor sit amet. Ut wisi enim ad minim veniam, quis nostrud exerci tation ullamcorper suscipit lobortis nisl ut aliquip ex ea commodo consequat.

Interests Ut wisi enim ad minim. Vel illum dolore eu feugiat nulla. Facilisis at vero eros et accumsan. Iusto odio.

Combination Résumé Sample

a targeted résumé may note positions, list experience, or give details that might not appear on any other document the applicant submits during a job search.

Although all résumés should "target" particular audiences in some way, conventional targeted résumés are appropriate for applicants who want to show immediate correlations between their training and experience and the needs and interests of a particular organization—even if the applicant would not offer this information to the industry at large.

Curriculum Vitae (CVs)

Roughly translated from Latin as "[the] course of [my] life," the curriculum vitae offers an applicant's employment history, qualifications for a job and, occasionally, personal information. European companies often ask job applicants to submit a curriculum vitae or "CV" but, in the United States, a curriculum vitae is frequently reserved for academic and medical careers.

Often running two or more pages, CVs offer comprehensive information about the applicant, including information about academic credentials (e.g., degrees, thesis titles and committee members), publications, presentations, committee work, professional contributions, and other job-related achievements that may not be valued in industry.

* * *

Whichever type(s) of résumé you find most appropriate for your purposes, you should review and, as necessary, update it every 2–3 weeks, while you can still recall discrete details about individual projects and their requirements. In doing so, you will be better prepared to share the most current list of your training and experiences on a moment's notice. But, of course, these same efforts will quickly reveal a downside: the space constraints of conventional résumés.

Faced with the challenge of keeping their résumés to a single page, many people simply delete information they consider obsolete, "dated," or less important than other, newer information in the résumés. Yet, while effective for the moment, such an approach can be short-sighted (especially if people are making all of these edits in a single file on their computer), because we never know when some of these earlier experiences may be of use later in our careers.

As such, you should resist completely expunging your work history—even when some experiences no longer seem relevant to your current or prospective positions. Instead, you should consider creating and maintaining a "Master Résumé" file for each résumé type you create.

A Master File résumé is a single, ever-evolving and growing document that includes the most comprehensive, yet concise and relative term-free description for *all* of the work you have done over the years—regardless of how many pages the file itself becomes. Then, as you submit applications, you would copy details (in full or in part) from various entries in the Master File résumé and paste them into an abridged, one-page version of your résumé for hard copy or electronic distribution. Similarly, you could cut and paste Master File résumé information into online-application systems for submission.

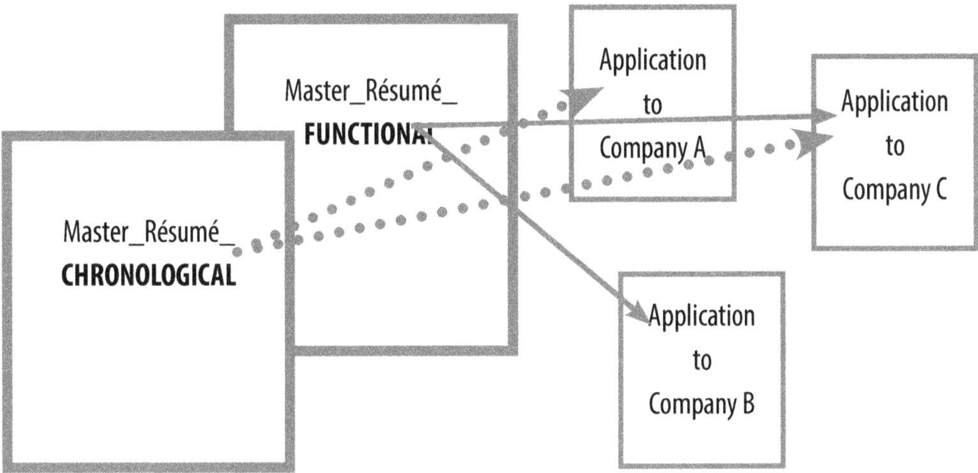

Creating a Master File résumé(s) can take time because you would need to review *all* of your earlier résumés and streamline the information into a single, comprehensive file. You might also include training, activities, experiences, and positions that have never appeared on your résumé, perhaps due to space constraints or because you may have decided these details did not correspond with your immediate or long-term professional goals. But, once your résumé's Master File is in place, and as it continues to grow, it can help you:

- conduct more focused career assessments with descriptions that identify strengths and areas for improvement in your skill sets.
- create more audience-appropriate résumés with details that appeal both to the industry at large and to a particular company,
- decide which information to include in a résumé, and which to put into an application letter,
- prepare for interviews as you consider your entire work history, even if particular elements no longer appear on your résumé, and
- update and distribute subsequent résumés in less time and with less anxiety by offering a single, centralized place for you to add and revise prospective résumé content during the "lulls" between job searches.

By maintaining this file—even after you have secured a position—you would also have a resource that could help you with performance reviews and salary negotiations. After all, this file would give you information describing the tasks you have completed, the projects you have pursued, the training you have received, skills you have improved, endeavors you have undertaken, value you have offered, and so on—all at your fingertips.

Furthermore, should you want or need to submit a résumé at a moment's notice, you would have complete, preformatted descriptions of your employment history to help you present the most current, concise, and accurate view of your abilities.

Exercise: Generating Your Master Résumé File

Because some experiences may no longer have an immediate correlation to the work you aim to do, creating a "Master Résumé" file would allow you to archive and locate all professional experiences, even as you acquire new talents and interests. Therefore, this exercise helps you set up a Master Résumé file, which you can add to and build upon in the months and years ahead.

Step 1. Locate and open the file for the most current version of your résumé, and give the file a new name that will help you identify it as your "go-to" source for the most current and complete résumé content and descriptions (for example, "Master_Résumé_Chronological.doc," or "Master_Résumé_Functional.doc").

Step 2. Review this file's content for training, positions, description details, and so on that may be missing, and start filling in the information. If you have earlier files or copies of your résumé, you might start by comparing the files' content and then copying and pasting all missing information from the earlier files into the Master File version of your résumé.

Step 3. Verify the completeness of each job description, even after synthesizing earlier versions of your résumé, and fill in the missing details.

Step 4. Consider information that may not have appeared on any résumé; this data might include miscellaneous jobs or positions and activities you may have considered inappropriate or unrelated to your target position. Add those details to your Master File.

Although the early stages of creating a Master File résumé may be primarily cutting and pasting information from different resources into a single file, the objective is to generate the most comprehensive, detailed record of your employment history. Therefore, in addition to reviewing previous application materials, you might consider reviewing employment records, pay stubs, photo albums, and other elements that can trigger your memory at different stages of your life. You might also revisit the Master File in general and individual sections or descriptions several times in the coming weeks or months to add details as you are able to remember them, especially since some details may be easier to recall during subsequent review.

Once you have brought your Master File résumé up to date with the most thorough explanation of every paid and unpaid position you have held, you should treat this file as a non-static document, one you revisit and update at least once a month. Doing so can ensure you always have the most current and complete version of your work history.

Exercise: Switching Formats and Increasing Options

Many job applicants create and stay with a single type of résumé throughout their professional lives, never knowing if another type—or even if a combination of formats—might be more effective. To see the possibilities, this exercise encourages you move beyond the "one-size-fits-all" résumé mentality.

Step 1. Locate and open the file for the most current version of your Master File résumé (or, for a smaller-scale version of this exercise, your most current résumé), and give it a new name to reflect an alternate résumé type.

Step 2. Reshuffle the content and details in your résumé to create either a functional/skills-based résumé (if you're presently using a reverse chronological résumé) or a reverse chronological résumé (if you're presently using a functional résumé).

Step 3. Consider information that might appear on your newly created, alternate résumé type that did not, or might not otherwise appear on the original résumé, and add that information.

Step 4. Compare the two versions of your résumé, identifying advantages and disadvantages of each. For example, does one version allow you to include information the other version does not? Do you gain or lose space with one version's descriptions? How might each résumé affect a reader's views of your skills and abilities?

Even if, ultimately, you never distribute the alternate résumé, completing this exercise offers another way to see and consider your skills; it also provides the foundation for creating complementary application materials.

Secret 11: Bullets can short-change an applicant's experience.

As they finalize the information to include on their résumés, job applicants must consider how they will lay out that information on the page. Unfortunately, prescriptive résumé guides, résumé templates, countless résumé samples available online, and ongoing debates about employer preferences regarding résumé formats that catch their eye are leading applicants to believe that résumés must incorporate bullets if they are to get any attention.

Bullets have become increasingly popular on résumés, and while bulleted lists can help a hiring manager quickly scan applicant details, being aware of the trade-offs concerning bullets can help you make the best decisions for presenting your credentials both fully and accurately.

In general, bullets call out select information. Therefore, bulleting each entry under a job description, in essence, highlights *everything*, making it harder for readers to distinguish the information of greatest importance on a résumé. Overusing bullets likewise creates a visual distraction, overwhelming hiring managers with 20–30+ instances of a single, monotonous symbol, each of which aims to attract the reader's full attention. Even following the advice of "selectively" using bullets raises questions about what information is best to emphasize—especially when other advice says a résumé must be consistent in formatting comparable information.

Another challenge of bullets is the resulting list. Although lists may be faster to read than paragraphs, lists suggest discrete, stand-alone elements, which can work against applicants trying to present a collection of interconnected experiences that, together, make a case for employment. Certainly their appearance under a single position may imply relationships between and among the isolated skills and abilities, yet lists themselves bring to mind miscellaneous, *ad hoc* activities, rather than a cohesive set of marketable expertise.

Perhaps the greatest disadvantage of bullets is the way bullets artificially lengthen the résumé, forcing applicants to make formatting choices that do not always serve them well. For instance, bulleted résumés place each entry on a new line—regardless of how long each individual line runs—requiring more space to present information, as evident in the following résumé excerpts. Notice how much space is required to present information in bulleted lists (see Version 1) when compared to presenting that same information—using identical typeface, type size, margins, and leading settings—in paragraph form (see Version 2).

Version 1

EXPERIENCE
California Nature Conservatory (CNC), Sacramento, CA
Human Resources Manager (October 2012 to present)

- Administer compensation, benefits and performance management systems, as well as safety and recreation programs
- Identify staff vacancies and work with appropriate teams to recruit, interview and select applicants
- Provide employees with information about policies, job duties, working conditions, wages, opportunities for promotion and employee benefits
- Analyze and modify compensation and benefits policies to establish competitive programs and ensure compliance with legal requirements

PowerHub Accounting, El Sobrante, CA
Accounting Clerk II (September 2010 to October 2012)

- Keyed daily worksheets to the general ledger
- Processed credit card payments and credits
- Prepared batch deposits
- Prepared requisitions for office, computer, and routine supply purchases
- Filed paid and unpaid invoices and statements

Accounting Clerk I (August 2009 to September 2010)

- Reviewed and maintained division's accounting records, including those that calculated expenditures, receipts, accounts payable and receivable, and profit and loss
- Prepared requisitions for office, computer, and routine supply purchases
- Reviewed invoices and bills to reconcile account statements
- Worked with other departments to obtain and convey fiscal information, ensuring accuracy of transactions between and among divisions

Contra Costa College, Rah-Rah Booster Club, San Pablo, CA
Volunteer (Fall seasons, 2007, 2009).

- Recorded transactions
- Managed accounts payable and receivable
- Reconciled bank statements

Version 2

EXPERIENCE

California Nature Conservatory (CNC), Sacramento, CA

Human Resources Manager (October 2012 to present). Administer compensation, benefits and performance management systems, as well as safety and recreation programs. Identify staff vacancies and work with appropriate teams to recruit, interview and select applicants. Provide employees with information about policies, job duties, working conditions, wages, opportunities for promotion and employee benefits. Analyze and modify compensation and benefits policies to establish competitive programs and ensure compliance with legal requirements.

PowerHub Accounting, El Sobrante, CA

Accounting Clerk II (September 2010 to October 2012). Keyed daily worksheets to the general ledger. Processed credit card payments and credits. Prepared batch deposits. Prepared requisitions for office, computer, and routine supply purchases. Filed paid and unpaid invoices and statements.

Accounting Clerk I (August 2009 to September 2010). Reviewed and maintained division's accounting records, including those that calculated expenditures, receipts, accounts payable and receivable, and profit and loss. Prepared requisitions for office, computer, and routine supply purchases. Reviewed invoices and bills to reconcile account statements. Worked with other departments to obtain and convey fiscal information, ensuring accuracy of transactions between and among divisions.

Contra Costa College, Rah-Rah Booster Club, San Pablo, CA

Volunteer (Fall seasons, 2007, 2008). Recorded transactions. Managed accounts payable and receivable. Reconciled bank statements.

As these examples demonstrate, bulleting information pushes résumé content further "down" the page. Thus, as applicants find themselves running out of space to present all of their experiences on a conventional one-page résumé, they often make additional formatting choices to compensate for the extra lines bulleted entries require.

One choice is to reduce the document's margins, adopting half-inch margins or smaller, thereby increasing the risk that the left and right edges of information may be cut off by printers that cannot accommodate borderless or full-bleed images.

Another format choice applicants make to compensate for the bullets in their résumés is to reduce the type size, opting for 8-point typeface (or smaller) and, thus, forcing readers to strain to read entries. Others turn to narrower typeface and tighter leading to pack as many words on the page as possible—usually at the expense of a reader-friendly, legible print presentation. Yet perhaps the most damaging choice applicants make to accommodate bulleted lists is deleting information from their résumé altogether.

By definition, résumés are abbreviated descriptions of a person's case for employment, but there's a difference between removing information because space constraints require all job applicants to select their strongest evidence for employment, and deleting information all together simply because a particular formatting decision minimizes space that might otherwise be available. By making format decisions that give you space to convey all that you need to say, you can offer hiring managers sufficient information to evaluate your application fully, and fairly.

This secret is not to suggest that using (or not using) bullets will result in any particular decision. Rather, it encourages you to select a format that can best present your qualifications for a given position. Hiring managers use résumés to identify what applicants can do to help the company meet its short-and long-term goals, and while some hiring managers may prefer to read résumés formatted in a particular way, even those with preferences have been known to interview applicants with alternately formatted résumés. After all, it isn't the résumé's format that conveys an applicant's qualifications; it's the content.

Considering that your application materials may be your only opportunity to showcase the expertise an organization wants to see in a prospective employee, you should start by deciding what information will help you make the strongest case for employment. Then, you should adopt a format that can accommodate all of that information in a reader-friendly manner.

Exercise: Bullets to Paragraphs, and Vice Versa

Many job applicants format their résumés according to what others say is the "best" or the "right" or the "only" way and remain convinced that the resulting format is the only option for them. This exercise encourages you to reformat your current résumé and examine the original and revised versions side-by-side to see which format—or combination of formats—can represent you most effectively on the market. For this exercise, you will need a hard copy and an electronic copy of your current résumé.

Version 1, Bullets to Paragraphs

If you are presently using *bullets* on your résumé...

Step 1. Open a copy of your résumé file and give it a new name, such as "Résumé_ParagraphFormatSample."

Step 2. Put a period at the end of each description in the résumé, if they presently do not exist.

Step 3. Remove paragraph returns and bullets from each description, creating paragraphs in which job descriptions are separated by a period. For example:

Before...

Gotham City College, Division of Computer & Technology, New York, NY
Assistant Director for Instructional Computing (January 20XX to May 20XY).

- Helped the Director coordinate programs and events in the campus's nine computer labs
- Worked with network administrator to ensure that the labs were operational at all times for its users
- Hired, coordinated, scheduled, and oversaw lab monitors
- Developed and oversaw software training workshops and general lab orientations throughout the year for faculty members and students
- Helped establish, convey, and maintain lab policies to ensure the labs could serve over 12,000 users each week
- Met with the campus's business manager and other Instructional Computer Committee members throughout the fiscal year to discuss short- and long-term upgrades for the computer lab

After...

Gotham City College, Division of Computer & Technology, New York, NY
Assistant Director for Instructional Computing (January 20XX to May 20XY). Helped the Director coordinate programs and events in the campus's nine computer labs. Worked with network administrator to ensure that the labs were operational at all times for its users. Hired, coordinated, scheduled, and oversaw lab monitors. Developed and oversaw software training workshops and general lab orientations throughout the year for faculty members and students. Helped establish, convey, and maintain lab policies to ensure the labs could serve over 12,000 users each week. Met with the campus's business manager and other Instructional Computer Committee members throughout the fiscal year to discuss short- and long-term upgrades for the computer lab.

Step 4. Reset margins to a conventional one-inch, and increase typeface to reader-friendly type size.

Step 5. Print out a copy of your newly formatted résumé and, comparing it to the hard copy of your original résumé, note advantages and disadvantages of each that can help you decide which version—or elements of each version—can best reflect your experiences to hiring managers:

___

___

___

___

___

___

___

___

___

Version 2, Paragraphs to Bullets

If you are presently using *paragraph* on your résumé…

Step 1. Open a copy of your résumé file and give it a new name, such as "Résumé_BulletFormatSample."

Step 2. Replace the periods separating each entry with a bullet.

Step 3. Insert a hard return before each bullet, starting each entry on a new line. For example:

Before…

HotButton Press, Detroit Michigan
Acquisitions Assistant (February 20XX to September 20XY). Acknowledged and recorded incoming folklore, music, popular culture, and anthropology manuscripts. Researched and solicited readers to evaluate works under consideration. Answered authors' questions about manuscript preparations and revisions. Devised method to track manuscript locations and evaluation return dates. Compared authors' revisions against original version of manuscripts to see that author addressed reviewers' concerns. Created concordances for complex, multi-version manuscripts to ensure accuracy in the texts for copy editors. Prepared manuscripts for copy editing and production stages. Verified that final manuscript, photographs, and permissions were on-hand for production cost estimates and copy editing. Researched potential markets for manuscripts to determine initial press-run figures. Wrote evaluations of incoming manuscripts and proposals for supervisor.

After…

HotButton Press, Detroit Michigan

Acquisitions Assistant (February 20XX to September 20XY)

• Acknowledged and recorded incoming folklore, music, popular culture, and anthropology manuscripts
• Researched and solicited readers to evaluate works under consideration
• Answered authors' questions about manuscript preparations and revisions
• Devised method to track manuscript locations and evaluation return dates
• Compared authors' revisions against original version of manuscripts to see that author addressed reviewers' concerns
• Created concordances for complex, multi-version manuscripts to ensure accuracy in the texts for copy editors

• Prepared manuscripts for copy editing and production stages
• Verified that final manuscript, photographs, and permissions were on-hand for production cost estimates and copy editing
• Researched potential markets for manuscripts to determine initial press-run figures.
• Wrote evaluations of incoming manuscripts and proposals for supervisor.

Step 4. Adjust margin settings to "hang" the bullets, aligning bullets to bullets and text to text.

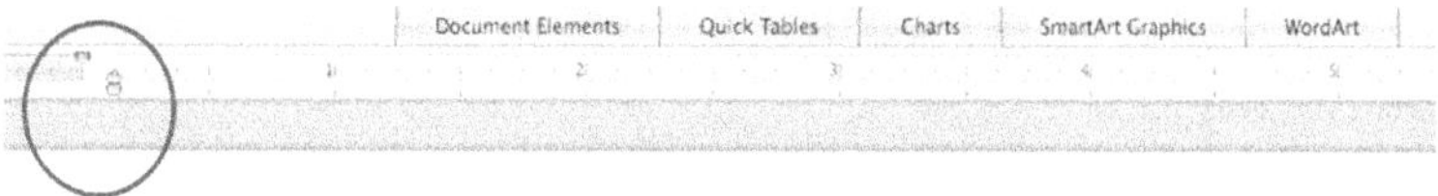

HotButton Press, Detroit Michigan
Acquisitions Assistant (February 20XX to September 20XY)

- Acknowledged and recorded incoming folklore, music, popular culture, and anthropology
- Researched and solicited readers to evaluate works under consideration
- Answered authors' questions about manuscript preparations and revisions
- Devised method to track manuscript locations and evaluation return dates
- Compared authors' re-visions against original version of manuscripts to see that author ad concerns
- Created concordances for complex, multi-version manuscripts to ensure ac-curacy in the t

Step 5. Print out a copy of your newly formatted résumé and, comparing it with your original résumé, note advantages and disadvantages of each that can help you decide which version—or elements of each version—can best reflect your experiences to hiring managers:

____

____

____

____

____

Secret 12: Elements that dangle, hover, or float can distract and misdirect attention.

Considering that most hiring managers spend, on average, 5–10 seconds reviewing an application, résumés must help the reader quickly find information about the applicant's credentials. The layout of a résumé can help in this endeavor by directing the reader's eyes to the most important elements on the page.

Whether those elements are the companies the applicant has worked for, the positions the applicant has held, the skills the applicant has to offer, or something else that demonstrates the applicant's credentials for the position, that information should be readily visible both to hiring managers who only glance at the page and to those who are willing to spend more time with the applicant's materials.

By deciding what information should be the center of interest or the outstanding unit of information, applicants can lay out their résumé in a way that helps a hiring manager see the most compelling evidence for why they are a match for the position—regardless of the time the hiring manager is willing to spend reviewing the document. It is for this reason that understanding how eyes move across a page can be of value.

Research shows that a reader typically "enters" the page on the left, usually near the top, perhaps because of conventional reading practices in Western culture. From there, the eyes travel to the most dominant element or detail on the page (the "focal point") and, unless held or redirected, continue to move downward and right, through information of less interest (the "field"), in preparation to "exit" the page, either moving through information at the bottom of the page (the "fringe"), or bypassing it all together.

The following images demonstrate these patterns in action.

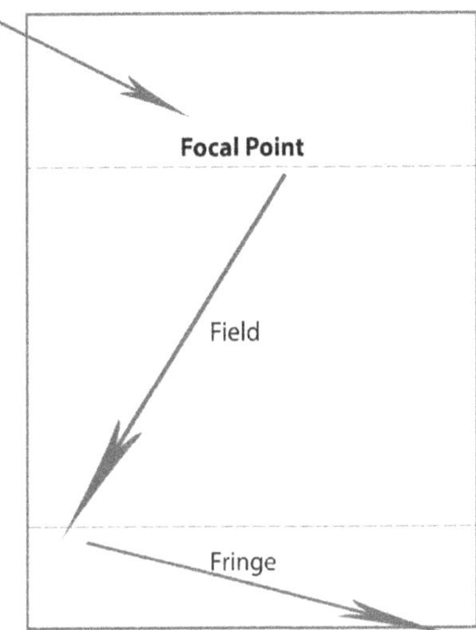

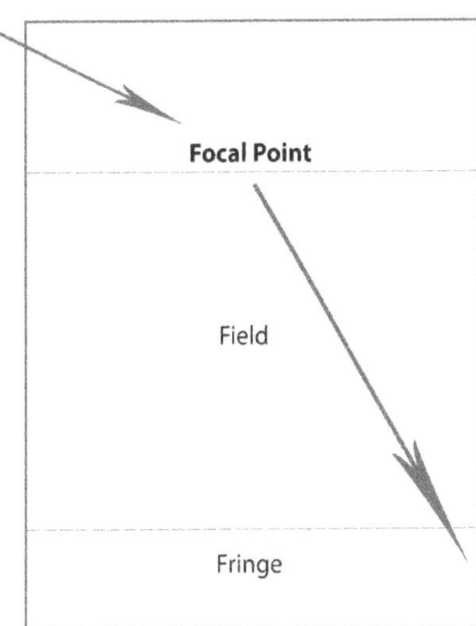

While designers may debate the values of layouts using Z-Patterns, F-Patterns, Guttenberg diagrams, and so on, job applicants should understand that the visual cues or signposts on their résumés (e.g., symbols, borders, headers and subheaders, indentations and alignment, character emphasis) can determine what attracts a reader's attention and, by extension, what a reader sees in the document.

Symbols and other pointing devices, for instance, have been used for years in advertising to draw a viewer's eyes to the most important elements in the layout. Although arrows and pointing fingers would guide a consumer's attention to coupons and products, nowadays an advertisement might use photographs, product illustration, and arrangement to lead the viewer's eyes toward particular content. In written documents, bullets provide a similar function, isolating and calling out details the author considers most important to notice; it is for this reason that bullets have become so popular on résumés.

Job applicants have come to believe that a hiring manager is more likely to "see" their experience with pointing devices "flagging" the reader's attention. Perhaps, but as explained in the previous secret, overwhelming readers with a single visual cue can undermine the impact of features meant to attract attention, prompting some applicants to use bullets only in particular sections of their résumé, or remove them completely. Even so, bullets offer one more example of how layout elements can affect how readers interact with a document.

The way information is organized can also affect a reader's interpretation of the information. Whether applicants choose to use a functional/skills-based résumé or a chronological résumé offers a case in point. Although the functional and chronological résumés would use identical (or near-identical) phrasing to describe the applicant's training and experience, grouping that information according to skills or sorting information according to position could ultimately affect how hiring managers see the applicant: is the applicant a compilation of skills, or is the applicant a product of environments in which he or she has worked?

This example demonstrates conceptual grouping, but there are also ways the organization of a résumé's content within a given format can affect a reader's interpretation.

In a chronological résumé, for example, some applicants choose to privilege the companies they have worked with, while others decide to privilege the positions they have held. These choices ultimately affect how information is presented and, therefore, emphasized. In the former case, the organization seems most important, subordinating the position (Example 1); in the latter case, the inverse would happen (Example 2).

Example 1, emphasizing the *organization*

COMPANY NAME, CITY, STATE
Position/Job Title (dates)

- Vel illum dolore eu feugiat nulla facilisis at vero eros et accumsan et iusto odio dignissim qui blandit praesent luptatum.
- Saril delenit augue duis dolore te feugait nulla facilisi.
- Sit amet consectetuer adipiscing elit, sed diam nonummy nibh euismod tincidunt ut laoreet.
- Adipiscing elit, sed diam nonummy nibh iriure dolor in hendrerit in vulputate velit esse molestie consequat.

COMPANY NAME, CITY, STATE
Position/Job Title (dates)

- Ut wisi enim ad minim veniam, quis nostrud exerci tation ullamcorper suscipit lobortis nisl ut aliquip ex ea commodo consequat.
- Consectetuer adipiscing elit, sed diam nonummy nibh euismod tincidunt ut laoreet dolore magna aliquam erat volutpat.
- Hendrerit in vulputate velit esse molestie consequat, vel illum dolore eu feugiat nulla facilisis at vero eros et accumsan et iusto odio.

Example 2, emphasizing the *position*

POSITION/JOB TITLE (dates)
Company Name, City, State

- Vel illum dolore eu feugiat nulla facilisis at vero eros et accumsan et iusto odio dignissim qui blandit praesent luptatum.
- Saril delenit augue duis dolore te feugait nulla facilisi.
- Sit amet consectetuer adipiscing elit, sed diam nonummy nibh euismod tincidunt ut laoreet.
- Adipiscing elit, sed diam nonummy nibh iriure dolor in hendrerit in vulputate velit esse molestie consequat.

POSITION/JOB TITLE (dates)
Company Name, City, State

- Ut wisi enim ad minim veniam, quis nostrud exerci tation ullamcorper suscipit lobortis nisl ut aliquip ex ea commodo consequat.
- Consectetuer adipiscing elit, sed diam nonummy nibh euismod tincidunt ut laoreet dolore magna aliquam erat volutpat.
- Hendrerit in vulputate velit esse molestie consequat, vel illum dolore eu feugiat nulla facilisis at vero eros et accumsan et iusto odio.

Sometimes, however, it is less about how an applicant sequences information than it is about visually displaying that information; such displays can include the typeface an applicant uses, as well as how the applicant groups, aligns, and indents elements on the résumé. To demonstrate, consider how an applicant might present his or her contact information:

Example 1

B.H. Delmyer
123 Main Street | Redmond, OR 97756 | 541.555.1212 | bhdelmyer@gmail.com

Example 2

B.H. DELMYER
123 Main Street,
Redmond, Oregon 97756
541-555-1212
email: bhdelmyer@gmail.com

Example 3

B.H. DELMYER
123 MAIN STREET, REDMOND, OREGON 97756
(541) 555-1212
EMAIL: BHDELMYER@GMAIL.COM

Example 4

B.H. DELMYER
123 Main Street, Redmond, Oregon 97756
541-555-1212
email: bhdelmyer@gmail.com

Although the content is the same, the way it appears on the document affects how readers "see" information and, thus, the applicant.

Applicants should also be attentive to the alignment of information on their résumés, paying particular attention to things that hang, dangle, hover, or float. For instance, "hanging" a résumé's category names in the left margin can help readers quickly scan and locate information categories of greatest interest, regardless of whether the résumé uses bullets or paragraph formatting.

EXPERIENCE

Position/Job Title
Company Name, City, State

- Dolor in hendrerit in vulputate velit esse molestie consequat, vel illum dolore eu feugiat nulla facilisis at vero
- Ut wisi enim ad minim veniam, quis nostrud exerci tation ullamcorper suscipit lobortis nisl ut aliquip ex ea commodo consequa
- Enim ad minim veniam, quis nostrud exerci tation ullamcorper suscipit lobortis nisl ut aliquip ex ea commodo consequa
- Elit esse molestie consequat, vel illum dolore eu feugiat nulla facilisis at vero
- Ad minim veniam, quis corper suscipit aliquip odo etrqua

Position/Job Title
Company Name, City, State

- Hendrerit in vulputate velit esse dolore eu feugiat nulla facilisis at vero
- Quis nostrud exerci tation ullamcorper lobortis nisl ut aliquip
- Nostrud exerci tation ullamcorper suscipit lobortis nisl ut aliquip ex ea commodo consequa
- Vel illum dolore eu feugiat nulla facilisis at vero
- Enim ad minim veniam, quis corper suscipit aliquip odo etrqua

Position/Job Title
Company Name, City, State

- Minim veniam, quis nostrud exerci velit esse molestie consequatation ullamcorper suscipit lobortis
- Nisl ut aliquip ex ea commodo consequa illum dolore eu feugiat nulla
- In vulputate facilisis at vero vel illum dolore eu feugiat nulla facilisis at vero
- Exerci tation ullamcorper suscipit lobortis nisl ex ea commodo consequa

* * *

EXPERIENCE

Company Name, City, State

Position/Job Title (dates). Dolor in hendrerit in vulputate velit esse molestie consequat, vel illum dolore eu feugiat nulla facilisis at vero. Ut wisi enim ad minim veniam, quis nostrud exerci tation ullamcorper suscipit lobortis nisl ut aliquip ex ea commodo consequa. Enim ad minim veniam, quis nostrud exerci tation ullamcorper suscipit lobortis nisl ut aliquip ex ea commodo consequa. Elit esse molestie consequat, vel illum dolore eu feugiat nulla facilisis at vero. Ad minim veniam, quis corper suscipit aliquip odo etrqua.

Company Name, City, State

Position/Job Title. (dates). Hendrerit in vulputate velit esse dolore eu feugiat nulla facilisis at vero. Quis nostrud exerci tation ullamcorper lobortis nisl ut aliquip. Nostrud exerci tation ullamcorper suscipit lobortis nisl ut aliquip ex ea commodo consequa. Vel illum dolore eu feugiat nulla facilisis at vero. Enim ad minim veniam, quis corper suscipit aliquip odo etrqua. …

In contrast, the oft-seen practice of "dangling" dates on the right (or left) margin can be a problem. Isolated and often "floating" in a margin, dates of employment can catch a reader's peripheral vision enough to redirect attention to information that is seldom the most compelling evidence for employment.

Centering information also makes information harder to locate than necessary, as does inserting larger-than-one-space gaps between bullets and the corresponding bulleted text. Such elements, increasing the numbers of indentations on the page, create visual hesitations for readers as they move across the document.

To demonstrate the effect of things that dangle, hover, and float, consider the following résumé layouts. Notice how the heading alignment, spacing, indentations, and so on in Version 1 force readers to work harder to identify relationships between and among the entries, working against a critical goal of a résumé: to show that various, potentially disparate training and abilities have prepared the applicant for a particular position.

Version 2, in contrast, presents the same information in the same typeface and type size; however, by minimizing the spaces, gaps, indentations, and the like, it creates a stronger visual cohesion—regardless of whether the résumé uses bullets or paragraph structure—helping readers focus on the most important information in the résumé.

Version 1

EXPERIENCE

POSITION/JOB TITLE *Company Name, City, State* dates

- Tincidunt ut laoreet dolore magna aliquam erat volutpat.
- Ut wisi enim ad minim veniam, quis nostrud exerci tation ullamcorper suscipit lobortis nisl ut aliquip ex ea commodo consequat.
- Duis autem vel eum iriure dolor in hendrerit in vulputate velit esse molestie consequat, vel illum dolore eu feugiat nulla facilisis at vero eros.
- Accumsan et iusto odio dignissim qui blandit praesent luptatum zzril delenit augue duis dolore te feugait nulla facilisi.
- Lorem ipsum dolor sit amet, consectetuer adipiscing elit, sed diam nonummy nibh euismod tincidunt ut laoreet dolore magna aliquam erat volutpat.
- Adipiscing elit, sed diam nonummy nibh iriure dolor in hendrerit in vulputate velit esse molestie consequat.

POSITION/JOB TITLE *Company Name, City, State* dates

- Vel illum dolore eu feugiat nulla facilisis at vero eros et accumsan et iusto odio dignissim qui blandit praesent luptatum.
- Saril delenit augue duis dolore te feugait nulla facilisi.
- Sit amet consectetuer adipiscing elit, sed diam nonummy nibh euismod tincidunt ut laoreet.
- Dolore magna aliquam erat volutpat.

POSITION/JOB TITLE *Company Name, City, State* dates

- Ut wisi enim ad minim veniam, quis nostrud exerci tation ullamcorper suscipit lobortis nisl ut aliquip ex ea commodo consequat.
- Consectetuer adipiscing elit, sed diam nonummy nibh euismod tincidunt ut laoreet dolore magna aliquam erat volutpat.
- Hendrerit in vulputate velit esse molestie consequat, vel illum dolore eu feugiat nulla facilisis at vero eros et accumsan et iusto odio.

RESEARCH

POSITION/JOB TITLE *Company Name, City, State* dates

- Dignissim qui blandit praesent luptatum zzril delenit augue duis dolore te feugait nulla facilisi.
- Uris nostrud exerci tation ullamcorper suscipit lobortis nisl ut aliquip.
- Commodo consequat eum iriure dolor in hendrerit.
- Vulputate velit esse molestie consequat, vel illum dolore, eu feugiat nulla facilisis at vero eros et accumsan et iusto odio.

Version 2, if using bullets

EXPERIENCE

POSITION/JOB TITLE *Company Name, City, State* (dates)
- Tincidunt ut laoreet dolore magna aliquam erat volutpat.
- Ut wisi enim ad minim veniam, quis nostrud exerci tation ullamcorper suscipit lobortis nisl ut aliquip ex ea commodo consequat.
- Duis autem vel eum iriure dolor in hendrerit in vulputate velit esse molestie consequat, vel illum dolore eu feugiat nulla facilisis at vero eros.
- Accumsan et iusto odio dignissim qui blandit praesent luptatum zzril delenit augue duis dolore te feugait nulla facilisi.
- Lorem ipsum dolor sit amet, consectetuer adipiscing elit, sed diam nonummy nibh euismod tincidunt ut laoreet dolore magna aliquam erat volutpat.
- Adipiscing elit, sed diam nonummy nibh iriure dolor in hendrerit in vulputate velit esse molestie consequat.

POSITION/JOB TITLE *Company Name, City, State* (dates)
- Vel illum dolore eu feugiat nulla facilisis at vero eros et accumsan et iusto odio dignissim qui blandit praesent luptatum.
- Saril delenit augue duis dolore te feugait nulla facilisi.
- Sit amet consectetuer adipiscing elit, sed diam nonummy nibh euismod tincidunt ut laoreet.
- Dolore magna aliquam erat volutpat.

POSITION/JOB TITLE *Company Name, City, State* (dates)
- Ut wisi enim ad minim veniam, quis nostrud exerci tation ullamcorper suscipit lobortis nisl ut aliquip ex ea commodo consequat.
- Consectetuer adipiscing elit, sed diam nonummy nibh euismod tincidunt ut laoreet dolore magna aliquam erat volutpat.
- Hendrerit in vulputate velit esse molestie consequat, vel illum dolore eu feugiat nulla facilisis at vero eros et accumsan et iusto odio.

RESEARCH

POSITION/JOB TITLE *Company Name, City, State* (dates)
- Dignissim qui blandit praesent luptatum zzril delenit augue duis dolore te feugait nulla facilisi.
- Uris nostrud exerci tation ullamcorper suscipit lobortis nisl ut aliquip.
- Commodo consequat eum iriure dolor in hendrerit.
- Vulputate velit esse molestie consequat, vel illum dolore, eu feugiat nulla facilisis at vero eros et accumsan et iusto odio.
- Commodo consequat eum iriure dolor in hendrerit.
- Vulputate velit esse molestie consequat, vel illum dolore, eu feugiat nulla facilisis at vero eros et accumsan et iusto odio.

Version 2, if using paragraphs

EXPERIENCE

POSITION/JOB TITLE *Company Name, City, State* (dates). Tincidunt ut laoreet dolore magna aliquam erat volutpat. Ut wisi enim ad minim veniam, quis nostrud exerci tation ullamcorper suscipit lobortis nisl ut aliquip ex ea commodo consequat. Duis autem vel eum iriure dolor in hendrerit in vulputate velit esse molestie consequat, vel illum dolore eu feugiat nulla facilisis at vero eros. Accumsan et iusto odio dignissim qui blandit praesent luptatum zzril delenit augue duis dolore te feugait nulla facilisi. Lorem ipsum dolor sit amet, consectetuer adipiscing elit, sed diam nonummy nibh euismod tincidunt ut laoreet dolore magna aliquam erat volutpat. Adipiscing elit, sed diam nonummy nibh iriure dolor in hendrerit in vulputate velit esse molestie consequat.

POSITION/JOB TITLE *Company Name, City, State* (dates). Vel illum dolore eu feugiat nulla facilisis at vero eros et accumsan et iusto odio dignissim qui blandit praesent luptatum. Saril delenit augue duis dolore te feugait nulla facilisi. Sit amet consectetuer adipiscing elit, sed diam nonummy nibh euismod tincidunt ut laoreet. Dolore magna aliquam erat volutpat.

POSITION/JOB TITLE *Company Name, City, State* (dates). Ut wisi enim ad minim veniam, quis nostrud exerci tation ullamcorper suscipit lobortis nisl ut aliquip ex ea commodo consequat. Consectetuer adipiscing elit, sed diam nonummy nibh euismod tincidunt ut laoreet dolore magna aliquam erat volutpat. Hendrerit in vulputate velit esse molestie consequat, vel illum dolore eu feugiat nulla facilisis at vero eros et accumsan et iusto odio.

RESEARCH

POSITION/JOB TITLE *Company Name, City, State* (dates). Dignissim qui blandit praesent luptatum zzril delenit augue duis dolore te feugait nulla facilisi. Uris nostrud exerci tation ullamcorper suscipit lobortis nisl ut aliquip.Commodo consequat eum iriure dolor in hendrerit.Vulputate velit esse molestie consequat, vel illum dolore, eu feugiat nulla facilisis at vero eros et accumsan et iusto odio.Commodo consequat eum iriure dolor in hendrerit. Vulputate velit esse molestie consequat, vel illum dolore, eu feugiat nulla facilisis at vero eros et accumsan et iusto odio.

Exercise: Making a Strong First Impression

This exercise helps identify what elements attract a reader's attention when seeing your résumé for the first time. You will need a copy of your résumé and a reader who is unfamiliar with your résumé's layout.

Step 1. Before showing your résumé, give the reader the following directions: "*I am going show you a copy of my résumé and, rather than ask you to read its content, I'm going to ask you to identify the first three things your eyes notice, no matter what they are.*"

Step 2. Move several feet away from the reader and hold up a copy of your résumé, allowing the reader to see the document's layout, but not necessarily read the descriptions. As an alternative, put your résumé on the floor and ask the reader to stand up or sit back until they can no longer read individual words.

Step 3. Ask the reader to identify what catches his or her attention first, second, third…, and then ask the reader to explain why these elements stood out.

1. ______________________________
2. ______________________________
3. ______________________________
4. ______________________________
5. ______________________________

Step 4. Consider whether the information the reader noticed is that which would make the best *first* impression on a hiring manager. If not, identify the information you would want a hiring manager to notice first, second, third…. Then, in the space below, note how to revise your résumé's layout so that readers would see that information more quickly and easily.

Step 5. Revise your résumé accordingly and repeat this exercise with another person, or two. Then move on to the next exercise.

Exercise: Tracking the Reader's Gaze

This exercise helps identify how readers might move through your résumé when they see it for the first time. You will need two copies of your résumé, a timer, and a reader who is willing to offer a guided tour of the journey through your résumé.

Step 1. Before turning over one copy of your résumé, give your reader the following directions: *"I am going to give you a copy of my résumé to review for an undisclosed amount of time. When the time is up, I will ask you to indicate where and how your eyes tended to move through the document. That is, where did your eyes look first, second, third, and so on. . . ."*

Step 2. Set the timer for 5 to 10 seconds or, if you're feeling generous, 15 seconds.

Step 3. Give one copy of your résumé to the reader and start the timer.

Step 4. When the timer goes off, ask the reader to walk you through the path their eyes moved, and in what order. Record the reader's path on your copy of the résumé.

Step 5. Consider the reader's eye movements and whether the resulting path is the one you would want a hiring manager to take when seeing your résumé for the first time.

Step 6. Identify how you would like readers to move through your résumé and list ways you could use elements of your résumé's layout to direct readers to the places you would like them to see first, second, third… in the space below.

____

____

____

____

Step 5. Revise your résumé and repeat this exercise with another person, or two, to ensure you are getting the results you would like. Then move on to the next exercise.

Exercise: Tightening the Dangling Elements

To offer readers the tightest, most visually cohesive presentation of information, review your résumé and identify all dangling, hovering and floating elements. Then tighten the visual presentation of your résumé by deleting extra spaces, removing multiple tabs, adjusting your document's alignment margins, and taking other steps to show stronger visual relationships between and among the elements on your résumé.

Secret 13: Formatting matters less than content.

In discussions of how to create or revise résumés, questions about formatting—the way information should appear on the page—inevitably emerge: What's the best font to use for a résumé? Is serif or sans serif typeface considered more professional? Can I mix typefaces? How small can my typeface be, and how narrow can I set my margins to accommodate everything I want to put on my résumé? Is it ever appropriate to underline information? Should I use ragged right or justified margins?...

While such questions eventually come into play, they are most effective at the *end* of the process—once job applicants decide what, exactly, they need to document in their résumés to demonstrate their qualifications for a particular position. Worrying about format before that point is like spending time making a report cover attractive, rather than making sure the report itself is complete, coherent, and audience-oriented.

The previous secrets address format considerations, but they do so to dislodge the idea that some résumé templates and formatting choices are inherently superior. Familiar is not necessarily better—especially when default format options require applicants to abbreviate or eliminate information about their training and experience in artificial ways.

Offering an abridged version of a person's training and experience, résumés must present an individual's credentials in the fewest possible words. But, again, there's a difference between presenting things concisely and eliminating information all together, assuming that hiring managers can or will be able to infer all an applicant can do.

Few people are hired simply because their résumés are attractive. Hiring managers want to know what applicants can do for them, and what your résumé says—not simply how it looks—will provide that information. By letting content determine your résumé's format, rather than letting a format dictate your résumé's content, you can give hiring managers a fuller, more accurate picture of what you can do and make a stronger case for employment.

Exercise: Making Conscientious Format Choices

Many job applicants adopt and settle upon a particular résumé format simply because of what they have seen or heard. Plugging their own experiences into a comparable design, applicants then use that format regardless of whether it is the best to convey their experiences to others.

Though your résumé may present your experiences to others, this exercise can help you verify whether its current format is the best or only format for your purposes. For this exercise, you will need a printout of your current résumé.

Step 1. Explain where and how you got the format for your résumé, along with any comments, advice, praise or caution you received regarding this layout, or elements within it:

____

____

____

____

____

____

Step 2. Identify the *advantages* you have found in explaining or presenting your experiences using the current format of your résumé:

____

____

____

____

____

____

Step 3. Identify any *disadvantages* you have found in explaining or presenting your experiences using the current format of your résumé:

____

____

____

____

____

____

____

Step 4. Note any training, experiences, information… you think prospective employers *should* know that is not presently represented on your résumé:

____

____

____

____

____

____

____

____

____

____

____

Step 5. Assuming that deleting information on your current résumé is *not* an option, list ways you could revise or reformat your résumé to accommodate the information you identified in Step 4:

Step 6. Create a résumé that incorporates the suggestions from Step 5. Before doing so, consider saving your current résumé as a new file with a different file name *before* incorporating the ideas and suggestions from Step 5, letting you compare the original and revised résumés more easily.

Step 7. Print out a copy of your revised résumé and, comparing it to the original, note advantages and disadvantages of each version.

In considering the original and newly created résumés side-by-side, you may see elements within each version that better reflect your abilities. In some cases you might prefer the newer version; in other cases, you might prefer the original version; you may even see ways to incorporate details from both versions into a third option.

Whichever version—or combination of versions—you choose, ideally you can see additional ways to present your training and experiences, rather than default to a particular format simply because *others* have said it's the way to go.

Congratulations! If you have moved through these secrets and completed the corresponding exercises, you are in a position to provide the most thorough, representative, and up-to-date version of your résumé at a moment's notice. The challenge will be *keeping* your résumé current and competitive.

Studies indicate that most people update or revise their résumés only when the opportunity (or need) for another position arises. This approach, however, works against even the most qualified applicants who must scramble to recall, articulate, and present their most recent training, experiences, and abilities—often in the midst of countless other responsibilities.

Adding to this dilemma is that most people tend to conflate several smaller tasks under larger, overly general descriptions, making it harder for someone without first-hand knowledge of the work to understand what, exactly, it took for the employee to complete the work in the context, with the resources, and in the time available. Thankfully, there is another way.

By developing the habit of updating your résumé or, more ideally, your Master Résumé file at least every month or so, you can generate résumés—as well as professional biographies, performance review content, and other information that relies on current descriptions of your efforts—with minimal lead time. The following exercise offers one way to develop this habit.

Exercise: Going on Record

This exercise can help you establish a system to both record what you do on a regular basis and generate complete, accurate descriptions of your experience in the most timely manner. For this exercise you will need a notebook, pad of paper, or other portable recording device.

Step 1. Schedule 5–10 minutes of uninterrupted time at the end of each work day. The actual times may fluctuate, but committing to a particular timeframe at the end of the day and adding it to your day's agenda will increase the likelihood that you will complete this task and develop the habit to sustain it.

Step 2. At the end of the day, during the appointed time, record in your notebook the work you did that day, regardless of whether you finished the task and regardless of how meaningful the work may seem in the larger scheme of things. If necessary, review professional calendars, emails, meeting notes, call records, project schedules, and other systems that document or otherwise reference what you have been doing and where you have spent your time. For example:

January 23

- Met with representative from Baker and Brewer to discuss increasing display booth order
- Answered emails and phone calls on event logistics from prospective sponsors
- Continued to solicit sponsors for back-of-the-room tables at keynote events; confirmed one publisher and generated leads on four others
- Followed up on budget approval status and notified all committee members of its delay. Made arrangements with printers to push back time program's production one week

- Participated in conference call with author and copyright lawyer to discuss using Heyller photographs in online promotions
- Interviewed two candidates for summer internship position

Step 3. At the *end of the week*, review the information you recorded throughout the week and generate tentative résumé descriptions that offer a concise, accurate, and complete representation of the work you have done. In doing so, resist combining and oversimplifying tasks into single descriptors. For example, rather than write "organized conference," identify the smaller tasks involved in that work: solicited and secured two sponsors; verified newly accepted panel members' acceptance and coordinated speaker schedules; visited and booked venue to accommodate 75–100 people; secured caterer, selected menu options, and sent contract to accounting for final approval; created and distributed invitations..."

Similarly, you might group several comparable tasks under a larger entry, such as "Responded to customer email and phone call inquiries about product information, order status, and billing concerns," or "Organized and facilitated meeting to review publication status of three manuscripts with each manuscript's acquisitions editor, copyeditor, and art director team, as well as the press's records manager and marketing manager to ensure all projects remain on schedule to meet target production deadlines."

Step 4. At the *end of each month*, review, edit, and streamline the tentative résumé descriptions and add the entries to your Master File résumé(s).

By generating, streamlining, and refining information while it's still available, familiar, or accessible, you will become more aware of details that best reflect your day-to-day work, which can help you generate a résumé on the spot.

These efforts can also help you explain the contributions you are making to the team, division, or larger organization whenever necessary, say when you are asking to be staffed on a particular project, negotiating a raise, or angling for a promotion. As importantly, as you recall and track work that has engaged and inspired you—and work that has not—you remain cognizant of and sensitive to tasks, projects, and opportunities you might want to pick up, decline, or renegotiate to move in directions that most interest you.

Part 3

Application Letters

As noted earlier, whereas résumés are industry specific, application letters are *company*-specific documents, which means applicants should write a unique letter for each organization to which they apply.

Certainly some of the information that appears in one application letter may appear in others, since a specific position may require a core set of skills, regardless of the employer. Even so, each organization may have distinct expectations and demands for how its employees do that work. Therefore, you can set yourself apart by writing letters that explain how the configuration of your training and experience can be of use to the specific company, showcasing your awareness of and, by extension, your interest in the particular organization

Although recruiters and head hunters may have personal preferences and biases when reviewing an applicant's materials, hiring managers generally agree that application letters with the following characteristics can damage the applicant's chances to secure an interview:

- **Too long**. Application letters should offer a one-page argument of how the applicant can be of service to the hiring manager's specific company.
- **Applicant-centric**. Application letters should focus on the company and how the applicant can help the organization meet its short- and long-term goals.
- **Weak, unclear opening**. Application letters should grab a hiring manager's attention without relying on artificial, contrived techniques.
- **Cryptic**. Application letters should explain the applicant's qualifications, rather than assume hiring managers can or will infer this information.
- **Superficially appealing**. Application letters should use concrete, verifiable details to demonstrate credentials.
- **Overly generic**. Application letters should explain how, why, and to what extent the applicant's experiences are relevant to the hiring manager's company.

- **Weak, disengaged closing.** Application letters should end on a confident, yet professional note to keep the application under active consideration.

- **Overwritten.** Application letters should convey applicant credentials in the most concise, precise manner.

- **Disorganized, incoherent, ungrammatical.** Application letters should demonstrate the applicant's technical competency for the position, as well as the applicant's proficiency in the conventions of written communication.

- **Misdirected.** Application letters should reach audiences who are in a position to make hiring decisions for the best review of materials.

Addressing these and other concerns hiring managers have about application letters, the secrets that follow offer strategies for generating precise, concise narratives that explain why you are qualified for the position you seek.

Secret 14: "Plug-n-chug" application letters can be deadly—especially in tight job markets.

Hiring managers want—and expect—applicants to make a case for why they are qualified to work in their company, yet most applicants write a single, catch-all application letter that focuses primarily, if not exclusively, on themselves, "personalizing" these letters in superficial ways. The most common method is the "plug-n'-chug" document.

In this type of document, applicants use word-processing software features to "find" the name, address, and target job title of one organization and "replace" them with the name, address, and job title of another company for each announcement they find. Although this approach helps people "write" and submit hundreds of applications with a few key strokes, the resulting mass-produced application letters are the equivalent of junk mail or spam, telling hiring managers the applicant isn't interested in *their* job, but simply *a* job.

As job hunters blanket the market with countless generic documents, hoping to find a match somewhere, hiring managers look for signs of applicants who can make knowledgeable contributions to *their* organization. Many of these signs appear during an interview, where applicants show what they know and don't know about the company by the answers they give, the comments they make, and the questions they ask. But application letters also reveal how much an applicant knows or cares about the particular organization and the work it does.

The following secrets explain how to move beyond the conventional plug-n-chug application letters that dominate the market. Before turning to these secrets, however, the next two exercises can help you determine whether the application letters you have been submitting may be more generic than ideal.

For these exercises, you will need a printout of an application letter you have been distributing (either through the mail or electronically), as well as a highlighter, color pencil, or color marker of your choice.

Exercise: The Salutation Test

The salutation (that is, the *Dear* _________: or *Dear* _________, portion of a letter or email) is often the first place readers look to see whether the document is, in fact, directed to them. It is precisely for this reason that generic salutations can work against job applicants, for the more generic the reference, the less familiar the applicant seems to be with the reader.

Using a scale of one to five, where "1" represents "No familiarity or awareness at all" and "5" represents "inner-circle alliance," look at your application letter's salutation and identify where it falls on the following familiarity continuum.

	Sample Salutations	Guidelines and Considerations
1	To Whom It May Concern:	Applicants may as well be writing "Dear Occupant." Consider how quickly messages addressed in such a manner can be dismissed if the reader were to say, "It doesn't concern *me*. . . ."
2	Dear Sir: Dear Sir or Madam: Dear Sir/Madam:	Better than "To Whom in May Concern," but still generic. It also makes it harder for the applicant to envision specific characteristics and interests of a hiring manager defined only by gender. It's like saying, "Hey, you! Listen up…"
3	Dear Hiring Manager: Dear HR Manager: Dear Hiring Committee: Dear Marketing Director: Dear Head of <division>	Professional default when the applicant doesn't have or know the hiring manager's name. Even if responding to job announcements with P.O. Box addresses or their equivalent, applicants can use the announcement for clues on the department or division overseeing the hiring process for potential title references.
4	Dear Elizabeth Doe: Dear Patrick Smith: Dear Yu-Ting Chen:	Professional option when the applicant has the hiring manager's name but has neither met that person, nor been explicitly invited to address the reader by his or her first name.
5	Dear Elizabeth: *or* Dear Liz: Dear Patrick: *or* Dear Pat: Dear Jonathan: *or* Dear Johnny: (if you have been invited to use reader's Anglicized name)	Professional familiarity matching that of an immediate peer or colleague. Presuming this familiarity can raise questions about the assumptions the applicant might make with clients and others who uphold conventional introduction etiquette—especially in an increasingly global economy, where different cultures have different protocols. Therefore, the applicant should use first-name and abbreviated name salutations *only* if the reader has given explicit permission to use these more familiar, collegial references.

More applications are being sorted electronically before human hands touch them, so specific names may not hold the same weight as they did in the past. Still, thinking about an actual human reading your letter can help you provide company-specific, reader-appropriate information.

If, for example, your application letter's salutation falls into either category 1 or 2, revise your salutation to help you envision a specific person, rather than a faceless entity, reading your application letter—someone with interests, likes, fears, passions, biases, and so forth that will inform what details stand out in applicant materials.

If your salutation falls into categories 3–5, you're on the right track. You should make sure, however, to verify the correct spelling of the reader's name. Even common, familiar names have unique spellings nowadays, and one misspelled word—especially in the reader's name—can be enough to remove an application from consideration.

Exercise: Spotting the "Plug-n-Chug" Application Letter

Even when the salutation is effective and appropriate, application letters can be overly generic based on how—or if—the letter references the target company. Using the same letter from the previous exercise:

Step 1. Highlight every reference to the company or organization with your highlighter, color pencil, or color marker of choice. Here, mark every reference to the reader's or company's name, as well as second-person references, such as *you* and *your*.

Step 2. Substitute the phrase "Surf's Up Sloppy Jo' Burger Joint," "Huntley's Tar and Gravel Supply" (or the name of an organization for which you would *not* want to work) for each reference to the target employer's name or company you highlighted in Step 1.

Step 3. Read the letter and ask if the information still makes sense, in full or in part—that is, *could* you submit this letter to the named company and still be considered a viable applicant?

Application letters in which the primary (or exclusive) focus is on the applicant tend to make sense regardless of which company or organization is being referenced, because such letters aren't about the particular company; they're about the applicant.

Considering that hiring managers want letters that reflect an awareness of and interest in *them*, the following secrets present ways to generate (or revise) your application letter so that hiring managers can see the talents *you* bring, but in ways *they* value.

Secret 15: Applicants can use the application letter's structure to highlight their qualifications to hiring managers.

Nowadays, especially in our highly digitalized world, people are uploading and submitting more application materials online, altering the expectations of both what job applicants should submit and what hiring managers might consider. Convention has dictated that individuals send a résumé *and* an application letter in response to every job posting but, as more announcements ask applicants to "submit a résumé," people increasingly believe that the application letter is optional, or even obsolete. Understand, however, that few hiring managers will spend time or energy guessing how your experience in the larger field or industry might transfer to their particular company. Thus, unless an application letter is explicitly forbidden, you should submit both a résumé and an application letter to strengthen your case for employment.

The following discussions explain how application letters can emphasize your credentials in ways that hiring managers value, starting with the letter's structure.

The Principle of Burying

To make strategic choices about the best places to present information in your application letter and elsewhere, it helps to understand the *Principle of Burying*, a communication strategy that uses an audience's varying levels of attention to advantage. Here's how it works.

Although its content and length may vary according to the purpose, audience, and context, information typically has a beginning, a middle, and an end. Given these parts, strategic communicators know that audiences are most attentive to information that comes at the beginning and at the end, and that audiences are least attentive to information that appears in the middle.

Take, for example, a speaker's presentation. People sitting in the audience will be most attentive in the early moments of the talk, as the speaker lays out the focus of the discussion. As the speaker continues, audience members may notice information here and there but, along the way, their attention may drift. Some people may begin to think about how they might use the information the speaker is offering; some may turn their attention to others in the audience or to the venue itself; some may be thinking about emails they need to write, people they need to call, deadlines they need to meet; and others may be thinking about their plans for dinner or for the weekend....

Suddenly, in the final moments of the presentation (usually signaled by the speaker saying something like, "In conclusion..."), audience members refocus their attention, waiting for the digest version of what they should take away from the presentation or how they might apply the information to best advantage.

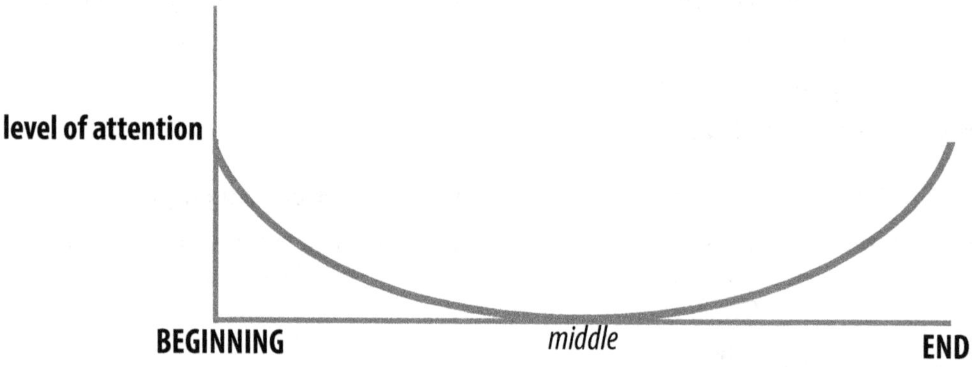

The same phenomenon happens in written documents, both in the larger sense and within the document itself.

Readers, for instance, are most attentive at the beginning (the introduction) and at the end (the conclusion) of documents, since the information in these locations typically outlines what the materials will cover, and what readers may need to do, respectively. In contrast, internal paragraphs often get a quick, cursory look—unless, of course, something within that area attracts the readers' attention.

Similarly, readers are more attentive at the beginning and end of sections and paragraphs, skimming information in between.

By keeping the Principle of Burying in mind as you write application letters, you can identify places a hiring manager may be more (or less) attentive while reading application materials and use that information to present your credentials in the most strategic places of a conventional application letter:

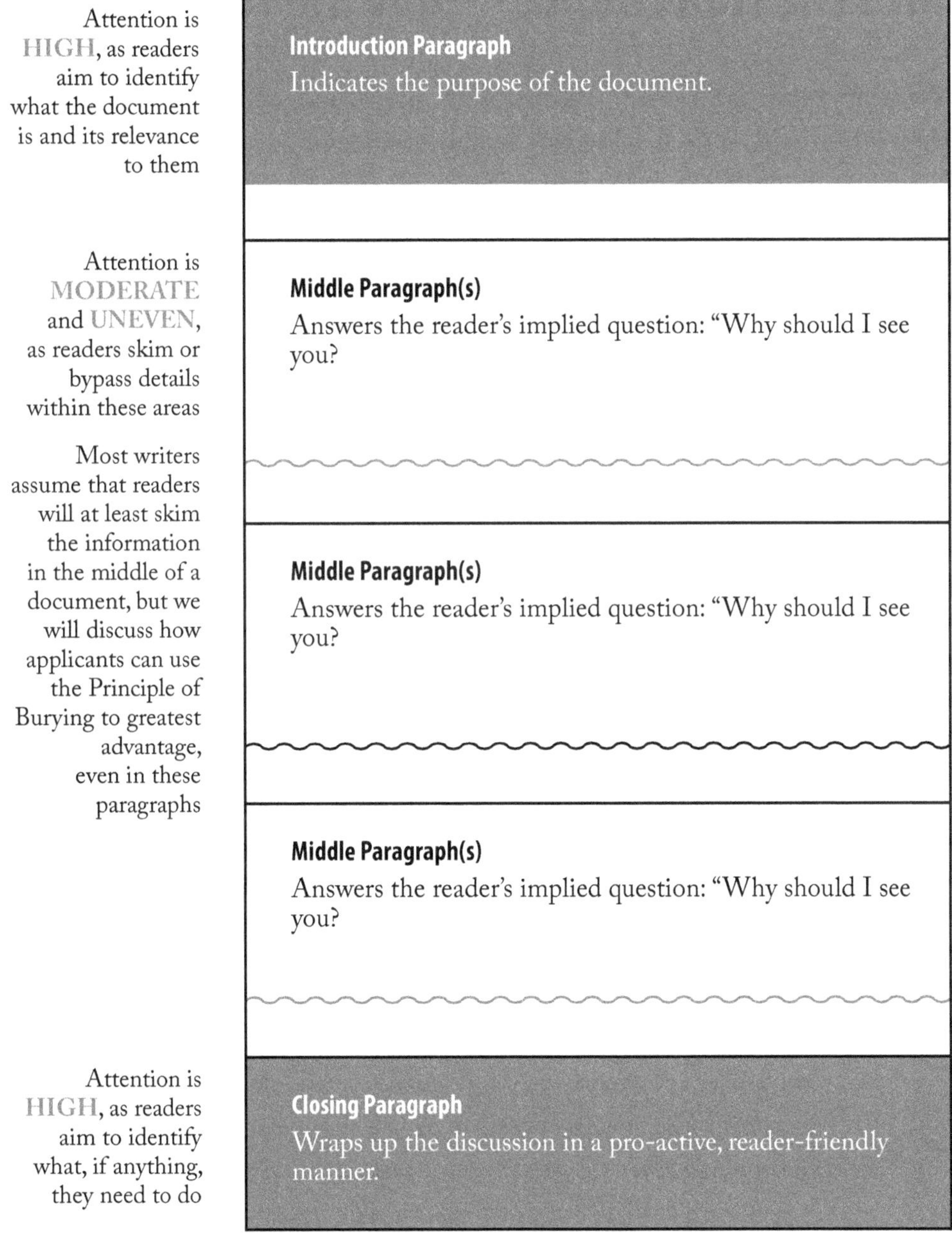

Attention is HIGH, as readers aim to identify what the document is and its relevance to them
Introduction Paragraph
Indicates the purpose of the document.
Attention is MODERATE and UNEVEN, as readers skim or bypass details within these areas
Most writers assume that readers will at least skim the information in the middle of a document, but we will discuss how applicants can use the Principle of Burying to greatest advantage, even in these paragraphs
Middle Paragraph(s)
Answers the reader's implied question: "Why should I see you?
Middle Paragraph(s)
Answers the reader's implied question: "Why should I see you?
Middle Paragraph(s)
Answers the reader's implied question: "Why should I see you?
Attention is HIGH, as readers aim to identify what, if anything, they need to do
Closing Paragraph
Wraps up the discussion in a pro-active, reader-friendly manner.

The following secrets explain how you can use each segment of the application-letter structure to stand out to hiring managers.

Secret 16: A concise, precise, targeted opening paragraph can put your application into the right hands—not the recycle bin.

Wanting to capture a hiring manager's attention, many job applicants begin their letters with superficial tactics, including metaphors (e.g., I am like the missing puzzle piece that will complete the image of your company…), personal anecdotes and narratives (e.g., Since I got my first Xbox, I have dreamed of working in the gaming industry…), textbook definitions (e.g., Marketing aims to sell products and services…), and industry pontifications (e.g., Current secular trends in the field of finance reveal that managers today must…). Unfortunately, what applicants may consider thought-provoking, surprising, or unique introductions to their credentials are often cliché story lines that have appeared in countless applications: I was lost, but now I'm found… I have overcome the odds, pulling myself up by the bootstraps… I can do amazing things for your company… I have a dream….

We only need to look at "real" application letters endlessly circulating online with snarky annotations by the letter's recipients and their coworkers to see that such openings seldom have the desired effect.

Considering that electronic and snail mail application materials inevitably arrive alongside countless other documents that demand a hiring manager's attention, your application letter should quickly, directly, and concisely identify the point of your message. You can do so by including the following information in your letter's opening paragraph:

- **The specific position you are applying for.**
  Companies may have several openings available at any one time. By identifying the specific position or job title you're applying for—as the organization refers to it—you can ensure the most appropriate readers within that organization evaluate your materials.

- **Position or job number references, if any.**
  Companies may have several openings with the same job title;

for instance, there may be a senior management position available both in Accounting and in Human Resources. By including a position or job number reference, when available, you can help hiring managers evaluate your qualifications within the context in which you aim to work.

- **Where or how you learned of the position.**
  Companies may advertise a position in several forums, each of which vets prospective candidates. If, for example, a job announcement appears in a national newspaper, the number of applicants applying for the position will be significantly larger than the number of applicants who may hear of the position through an alumni network, community job fair, or current employee. By specifying how you learned of the position, you may find a more favorable reception for your materials.

- **When you might be available, if not immediately.**
  Companies generally assume job applicants are available immediately, or they can be with a conventional "two week notice." Some positions, however, may be advertised weeks or even months in advance. Jobs in academia, for instance, may be advertised months before a school year starts; similarly, entry-level positions for new college graduates may be filled a semester or two prior to the students' graduation.

  There may also be times when the person applying for a position cannot be available immediately, either because of industry cycles (e.g., seasonal employment opportunities) or because of other commitments with a definitive ending. In such cases, you may find it more strategic to identify tentative start times up front, saving the hiring manager, and yourself, time.

The following samples show how all of this information might come together precisely and concisely in the opening paragraph of an application letter. And, yes, single-sentence opening paragraphs are both possible and appropriate.

I am applying for the position of Financial Analyst Supervisor II (Job ID # 12357), posted on your company's website.

Thank you for talking with me about Byron, Inc.'s new office in Fremont. Thinking more about our conversation and the opportunities you mentioned, I am applying for the position of Marketing Specialist.

After speaking with your company's representatives, Erica Tzu and J.D. Mueller, at the Blarney City Networking event on June 21, 20XX, I am applying for the Client Services Administrator position.

Graduating next December with a degree in criminal justice from the University of Missouri–St. Louis, I am applying for one of the student internships in the U.S. Attorney's Office for the spring 20XX semester.

As a junior in Library Science with an interest in digital archiving, I became aware of the Smithsonian Institution Libraries In-Residence Program while attending a workshop on archives in the Capital Gallery. Reading more about the In-Residence Program on your website and seeing the options available to undergraduates, I am applying for a semester or year-long appointment in the Digital Library and Information Systems division, starting Fall 20XX.

Julie Nigel, Director of Accounting in your office, suggested I write to you about opportunities in your group. Graduating with a degree in advertising from the University of Texas this May, I am applying for an entry-level position in the Marketing Division.

On November 3, 20XX, a representative from your organization spoke to our division about employment opportunities in the Miami office. As a Staffer in the Daytona branch, I have developed skills that could be of service to Managing Directors and their teams, prompting my application to the Real Estate group in your office.

> As requested during our meeting on Friday, April 23, this letter chronicles my experience in acquisitions as part of my application for the 20XX Summer Internship at Brower Press.

As these examples demonstrate, identifying the position, job numbers, how you learned about the position and, if necessary, your availability makes it easier for a hiring manager to know what, exactly, the letter is about, instantly contextualizing the discussion. Equally important is that this information, appearing in one or two sentences, demonstrates your awareness of and respect for the reader's time.

Finally, the information sets up the subsequent middle paragraphs, which present a case for why the hiring manager should talk to you.

Exercise: Creating a Company-Specific Opening Paragraph

To start your application letter in a professional, reader-oriented manner, you will need logistical information about the position for which you are applying; that information typically appears in the job announcement.

Step 1. Record the following information about the position you are applying for:

- ❑ *Name of the specific position/title:* ______________________

  ____

- ❑ *Position/Job number references, if any:* ______________________

  ____

- ❑ *List all of the places and resources from which you learned about this position's availability, using exact name(s), dates, references… when available* (e.g., newspaper and publication date, website and its sponsor; particular job forum; target company's website; company employee or affiliate, along with that person's name and title; any combination of these resources)

  ____

  ____

  ____

  ____

  ____

  ____

- ❑ *When you might be available, if not immediately:* ________

  ____

Step 2. Incorporating the details from Step 1, write one or two sentences to help a hiring manager identify the overall purpose of your letter—to apply for a position in the reader's organization:

You now have the opening paragraph for a company-specific application letter, setting up the paragraphs where you demonstrate your credibility as an applicant, as the next two secrets explain.

Secret 17: (Seemingly) Ego-centric applicants struggle to get an audience with prospective employers.

Although job applicants are most interested in what they will get from a position, hiring managers are most concerned with how *they* will benefit from the hire. And while there are several ways hiring managers can distinguish applicants who seem more (or less) interested in helping their company succeed, one of the most immediate indicators is how often applicants refer to themselves during the process, as the following exercises demonstrate.

Exercise: The "I's" Have It…

For this exercise, you will talk with someone you know for 3–5 minutes. The topic(s) you address during this conversation is up to the two of you. The only restriction is that neither of you can use the following words (or their non-English equivalent): *I*, *Me*, *My*, and *Mine*.

Step 1. Write the words *I*, *Me*, *My*, and *Mine* (or their non-English equivalent) on a sheet of paper for each participant's reference.

Step 2. Set a timer for 3–5 minutes.

Step 3. Begin a conversation on a topic of your choice, calling out each time someone says *I*, *Me*, *My*, or *Mine*.

After the buzzer sounds, take 5–10 minutes to record the observations you and your conversation partner have about the interaction. In doing so, you might consider: How easy or challenging was it to get the conversation started, or to sustain the discussion? What helped or hindered the conversation for each speaker? What did each participant do to overcome the conversation hurdles he or she encountered? How "natural" did these actions feel during the exchange?

Exercise: The "I's" Have It . . ., Variation

As an alternative to the exercise above, observe another couple's conversations for 3–5 minutes, and the ways their communication is affected by the use, or non-use, of the words *I*, *Me*, *My*, and *Mine* (or their non-English equivalents).

Step 1. Divide a sheet of paper in half and record each participant's name at the top of each column.

Step 2. Write the words *I*, *Me*, *My*, and *Mine* on a separate sheet of paper for the participants' reference.

Step 3. Instruct participants that they can discuss any topic(s) they choose, but they cannot use the words on the sheet of paper (i.e., *I*, *Me*, *My*, and *Mine*) during the conversation.

Step 4. Set a timer for 3–5 minutes, and ask the participants to begin.

Step 5. Document each time one of the participants uses *I*, *Me*, *My*, and *Mine* (or their non-English equivalent) with a hash mark or some other indication below the speaker's name, as well as other communication cues (e.g., body language, facial expressions, pitch, pace, pauses) for each participant when they use, or hear, these words.

Step 6. After the timer goes off, ask the participants for their observations about the conversation. For example, how easy or challenging did they find it to get the conversation started, or to sustain the discussion? What helped or hindered the conversation for each speaker? What did each participant do to overcome the conversation hurdles he or she encountered? How "natural" did these actions feel during the exchange?

Step 7. Share your own observations about their conversation and ask the participants if their impressions of the conversation change in light of the observations you share.

* * *

These exercise demonstrate the difficulty many people have when they are unable to talk about themselves, even briefly. We are selfish individuals, interested in the world from *our* points of view, and *we* want to share *our* points of view with others. Even when listening to other speakers, *we* often hear and interpret information through the filters *we* deem important, wondering how *we* can use the information to best advantage. The insights *we* have, in turn, compel us to share *our* ideas, perhaps becoming impatient waiting for *our* turn; after all, *we* tell ourselves, *our* thoughts and observations are relevant, important, and interesting, and others will clearly benefit from what *we* have to say....

The desire to share ideas, perspectives, thoughts and opinions is not necessarily a negative, but we should recognize that the more we focus on ourselves, the less we focus on others, even inadvertently; this imbalance can become a problem, especially in the job search. Specifically, when applicants focus mostly—or primarily—on themselves and what *they* will get from the job, they inevitably are less attentive to the company and how the *company* can be better off by hiring them.

To be clear, this discussion does *not* suggest you avoid talking about yourself; you must talk about yourself and your credentials to make a case for employment. However, you should be attentive to where, how, and how often you may be talking about yourself at the expense of a company looking to hire someone that can satisfy *its* needs and interests. It's a subtle difference, perhaps, but a critical one—especially in a context where applicants are trying to make a solid first impression, as the next exercise demonstrates.

Exercise: First Impressions

Imagine that you are a hiring manager looking at materials from prospective applicants when you come across the following application letter. Because you have a stack of applications to review before lunch, you decide to read the letter quickly and record your initial impressions to help decide whether this applicant deserves further consideration.

> Dear Hiring Manager:
>
> I am applying for the position you advertised on www.jobbank.com.
>
> Having seen your advertisement for an opening in your company, I believe I can bring much to your organization. I have diverse experience in the field, as well as extensive leadership experience to offer. My most recent work experience was as a sales representative for Empire Reserves, where I assisted a range of teams in analyzing the best markets for potential prospects. I was instrumental in my team's ability to promote several main and peripheral products to our clients, and I have received numerous commendations from peers and supervisors verifying to my contributions to the company's efforts.
>
> I also bring a passion for problem solving. My experiences at EMT Services were both challenging and exciting, and an aspect of the job I found most rewarding was working closely with intelligent individuals who were dedicated to their work. I have learned much from them and, in the process, I have acquired both an appreciation for the difficulties companies face in meeting client needs and an excitement for the myriad creative solutions possible to meet those needs. This experience has strengthened my interest in customer service, and it has given me expertise I can bring to your company.
>
> My excellent communication abilities can also be of service to your firm. I regularly deliver pitch presentations and

have been active in Toastmasters since 2013. My work in ABC organization has also helped me hone my abilities to communicate clearly and effectively with others; it's also helped me strengthen my abilities to delegate tasks, manage time, and promote an organization.

In addition to my communication abilities, I can type 75 wpm and use a Microsoft Word, Excel, ClarisWorks, and PowerPoint. I also work well with people and have participated in several team projects, showing my ability to work both independently and as part of a team.

I am confident that I can meet the expectations you hold for incoming employees, and I believe that I would be a valuable addition if given the opportunity. I have enclosed a copy of my résumé so you can read more about the experiences and skills I could offer your company, and I would welcome the chance to talk more about the ways I can be of service to you. Please call me at (XXX) XXX-XXXX so we can talk further. Thank you.

Sincerely,

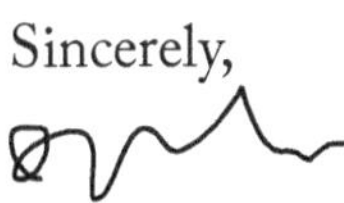

J.P. Candidate

First impressions and observations about the applicant ...

____

____

____

____

____

____

Having read this letter, you may have found that the applicant has experience that could be of use to several organizations, including your own. Furthermore, because the letter explains where and how the applicant acquired that experience, you may be able to envision places this person could fit into your organization.

Such favorable impressions can serve the applicant well but, upon closer examination, you might notice that something is missing: information indicating what, if anything, the writer knows about *your* organization. In fact, every reference to your company is overly general and generic, as the following version demonstrates; references to the applicant are in bold italics, and references to the company are underlined:

> Dear <u>Hiring Manager</u>:
>
> ***I*** am applying for the position <u>you</u> advertised on www.jobbank.com.
>
> Having seen <u>*your*</u> advertisement for an opening in <u>your</u> company, ***I*** believe ***I*** can bring much to <u>your organization</u>. ***I*** have diverse experience in the field, as well as extensive leadership experience to offer. ***My*** most recent work experience was as a sales representative for Empire Reserves, where ***I*** assisted a range of teams in analyzing the best markets for potential prospects. ***I*** was instrumental in ***my*** team's ability to promote several main and peripheral products to our clients, and ***I*** have received numerous commendations from peers and supervisors verifying to ***my*** contributions to the company's efforts.
>
> ***I*** also bring a passion for problem solving. ***My*** experiences at EMT Services were both challenging and exciting, and an aspect of the job ***I*** found most rewarding was working closely with intelligent individuals who were dedicated to their work. ***I*** have learned much from them and, in the process, ***I*** have acquired both an appreciation for the difficulties companies face in meeting client needs and an excitement for the myriad creative solutions possible to meet those needs. This experience

has strengthened ***my*** interest in customer service, and it has given ***me*** expertise ***I*** can bring to your company.

My excellent communication abilities can also be of service to your firm. ***I*** regularly deliver pitch presentations and have been active in Toastmasters since 2013. ***My*** work in ABC organization has likewise helped ***me*** hone ***my*** abilities to communicate clearly and effectively with others; it's also helped ***me*** strengthen ***my*** abilities to delegate tasks, manage time, and promote an organization.

In addition to ***my*** communication abilities, ***I*** can type 75 wpm and use a Microsoft Word, Excel, ClarisWorks, and PowerPoint. ***I*** also work well with people and have participated in several team projects, showing ***my*** ability to work both independently and as part of a team.

I am confident that ***I*** can meet the expectations you hold for incoming employees, and ***I*** believe that ***I*** would be a valuable addition if given the opportunity. ***I*** have enclosed a copy of ***my*** résumé so you can read more about the experiences and skills ***I*** could offer your company, and ***I*** would welcome the chance to talk more about the ways ***I*** can be of service to you. Please call ***me*** at (XXX) XXX-XXXX so we can talk further. Thank you.

Sincerely,

J. P. Candidate

In looking at the number, placement, and content of the highlighted items, we can identify elements that may affect a hiring manager's views of the applicant, even subconsciously, including:

- **Number and proportion of references.**
  The number of references to the applicant in this letter (especially when compared to the number of references to the company) focuses every discussion on the applicant—at the expense of the company.

Again, applicants need to talk about themselves and their experiences, but when discussions are overwhelmingly tipped in favor of the applicant, hiring managers will struggle to see themselves and their companies in the discussion.

Considering that hiring managers are most concerned with what *they* will get from the hire, applicant-centric letters will have more difficulty making a case for employment. Even combining and condensing sentences and clauses to minimize the number of references to the applicant could downplay the effect of writer-centric documents, at least visually.

- **Location of references.**
  Most of the references to the applicant in this letter are at the beginning of sentences and paragraphs, while references to the company are generally tucked into the middle of sentences and paragraphs. According to the Principles of Burying, the locations of these references consistently put the applicant at the center of attention and the company on the sidelines.

- **Grammatical emphasis of references.**
  Most of the references to the applicant in this document are the grammatical subject of the sentence; in contrast, references to the company are grammatical objects. Considering that grammatical subjects carry the weight of the sentence—noting who or what is the main topic—the sentence structures of this document reinforce that the applicant is the primary focus of this conversation, while the company is peripheral at best.

In addition to these elements, this letter relies on overly-generic references to the reader's company. While this tactic would allow the applicant to distribute this same letter to countless other organizations, it also suggests the applicant knows little or nothing about any particular organization's needs and interests.

Few hiring managers will dissect application letters to this degree, but most feel the effect of an applicant-focused, plug-n-chug letter: The applicant isn't interested in what *this* company does, or how; the applicant is simply looking for *a* job.

The next secret explains how to create more company-sensitive application documents. If, however, you have an application letter that you've been submitting as part of your job application, complete the following exercise to identify the impression your letter may be making on its recipient(s).

Exercise: What Color Dominates?

To identify the focus of your application letter, you will need a hard copy of an application letter (either one you submitted by email or by snail mail), as well as two highlighters, color pencils, or color markers of your choice.

Step 1. Fill in each circle with a different color, assigning one color to each of the following elements: references to yourself (the applicant), and references to the reader (the prospective employer).

1 = first-person references to me, the applicant (e.g., *I*, *me*, *my*, *mine*)

2 = second-person references to the reader (e.g., *you*, *your*, *yours*), as well as reference to the reader's or company's name

Step 2. Locate first- and second-person references in your application letter, and color-code each reference with its respective color.

Step 3. Look at the number and locations of each color—in isolation, as well as in proximity to and proportion with the other color—to identify who is the focus of sentences, paragraphs, the larger document.

This exercise will not generate a prescriptive list of things you should or must "fix" in your application materials. It simply highlights—figuratively and literally—the focus of your current application letter in preparation for the next discussion, which will examine how to make your case for employment in ways that stand out to hiring managers.

Secret 18: Using the "You–Me–Us" approach in the middle paragraphs of an application letter can downplay even the most (seemingly) ego-centric applicant.

Often job searches are broken into "us" versus "them" discussions. There are companies with positions to fill, and there are job applicants looking for a job, and whether someone is classified as "us" or "them" depends on which side of the interview desk the person sits. Rather than adopting a two-party mentality, effective job applicants must envision *three* characters in the discussion:

You The hiring manager/company with particular needs and interests, prompting a job opening.

Me The job applicant needing to demonstrate the ability to do the work the company has.

Us A combination of the "You" and "Me" characters at the conclusion of the search, enhancing the position and status of *both* parties.

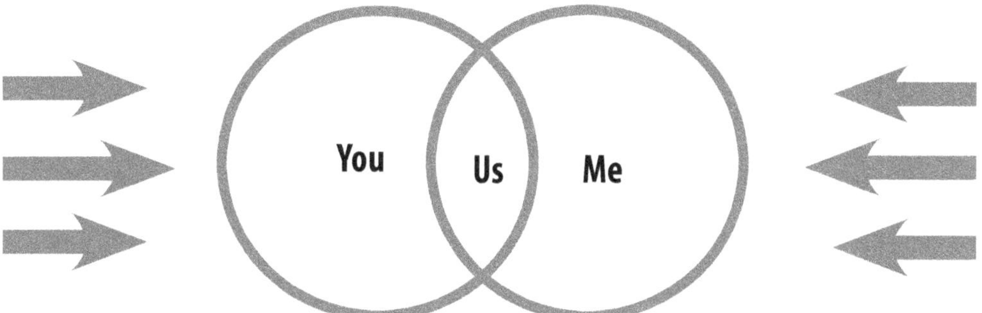

The "You–Me–Us" approach to writing application letters engages all of these characters by offering character-appropriate information in strategic places, and in strategic ways.

To best understand this approach, it helps to distinguish between solicited and unsolicited job applications.

Solicited applications are those in which a company announces a position's availability and, in doing so, invites individuals to apply. These job announcements typically indicate what a company wants done, as well as what applicants need to do that work.

Unsolicited applications, in contrast, are initiated by individuals who contact an organization to offer their services; whether a company would be willing to consider the person for any future openings, or even create a position to bring the individual on board, depends on the need that person has been able to identify and propose filling.

Type of Application	Reader Expectation	Reader's (Initial) Reception
Solicited	expected	favorable → neutral
Unsolicited	unexpected or even unwanted	neutral → hesitant → hostile

Of the two, solicited application letters are generally easier to write. After all, applicants not only face a more receptive audience, but they can know up front what the company is actually looking for in candidates because job announcements often provide the company's "wish list" of applicant qualifications. Therefore, the applicants who can speak to those qualifications would be—at least on paper—more viable than those who cannot.

Still, applicants must do more than claim they have the qualifications a company seeks; they must be able to verify those qualifications in context and, ideally, demonstrate an awareness of where and how those qualifications could help the company meet its short-and long-term goals. This connection is the foundation of the "You–Me–Us" approach.

To demonstrate this concept, we'll consider how someone might apply for a Regional Sales Manger position, using information from the following job announcement:

HELP WANTED

Regional Sales Manager (US and Canada)
The Journals Division of Nance & Talley, a leading publisher in the biological sciences, has an excellent opportunity for a dynamic sales professional to join its growing sales team. Reporting to the Director of Journals Sales, the successful applicant will be responsible for the development and management of online sales throughout the United States and Canada.

Responsibilities: Increase and promote sales of print and online journals throughout assigned region; identify and pursue opportunities for growth and development; negotiate and execute sales agreements; produce monthly reports on activity and development; assist in the development of sale proposals, management reports, supporting sales contact/CRM database; manage and train Journal Sales Executive and supporting staff; and, attend library meetings and industry events, as required.

Qualifications: Excellent organizational and project management skills with the demonstrated ability to manage and train staff. Must be able to handle multiple projects and deadlines simultaneously. Excellent written and verbal communication skills and advanced presentation skills at all levels of business. Must have effective account management skills. The ability to develop relationships and partnerships, both internally and externally, is critical. Fluency in French is preferred.

Requirements: Bachelor's degree, preferably in a biological science. At least five years sales experience in academic publishing with previous management and training experience. Proficiency with Windows, including MS Word, PowerPoint, and Excel; CRM software required. Domestic and international travel is required.

About Nance & Talley: Founded in 1989, Nance & Talley has become a leading international publisher of journals and textbooks emphasizing the biological sciences With offices in 15 countries, N&T specializes in human embryology, genetics, microbiology, and molecular biology. Its list presently includes over 450 active textbook and 25 active journal titles.

Although advertising for a sales manager, this job announcement is fairly conventional. It offers an overview of the company, explains what it does in general, describes what the employee would be doing, and provides a list of training and experience the company seeks in the applicants it would hire to perform those tasks. In the process, this and comparable announcements provide critical information for the "You" and "Us" portions of the "You–Me–Us" approach, which may be easier to see when details from the job announcement are mapped into a "You–Me–Us Brainstorming Chart."

The "You–Me–Us Brainstorming Chart" is a tool for summarizing and synthesizing key details about a job opening's requirements and a prospective applicant's offerings. By completing this chart, applicants can strategically identify where, how, and to what extent their experience and training may correlate with the target company's needs and interests, as is evident in the way someone interested in the Nance & Talley Regional Sales Manager position might complete the chart.

You–Me–Us Brainstorming Chart, Sample

Company Name and Address:	Nance & Talley 1234 Main Street Wichita Falls, TX 76308	
Position and, if available, any reference numbers:	Regional Sales Manager	
Where/How learned about position:	*Chronicle of Higher Education*, online job database (November 1, 20XX)	
"YOU" Wish-List of Characteristics Here, insert applicant qualifications called out in the company's job announcement	**"ME" "Proof" you have characteristic** Here, list the specific positions, activities, training, experiences, degrees, classes and workshops, and other tangible practices demonstrating you have the desired characteristic or skill (consult your résumé and other application materials for ideas)	**"US" Transferability Factor** Here, identify ways you could use or apply this skill in the target company's construction of the position; incorporate details you acquired by researching the company, networking…
LEADERSHIP/ MANAGEMENT: • demonstrated ability to manage and train staff. • previous management and training experience.		• manage and train Journal Sales Executive and supporting staff
ORGANIZATION/TIME MANAGEMENT: • effective account management skills. • excellent organizational & project management skills. • able to handle multiple projects and deadlines simultaneously.		• produce monthly reports on activity and development • assist in the development of sales proposals, management reports, supporting sales contact/CRM database

COMMUNICATION/ SALES: • excellent written/verbal communication skills. • advanced presentation skills at all levels of business. • fluency in French (pref). • at least five years sales experience in academic publishing. • proficiency with Windows, including MS Word, PowerPoint, and Excel; CRM software required.		• develop relationships and partnerships, both internally and externally • negotiate and execute sales agreements; • increase and promote sales of print and online journals throughout assigned region • pursue opportunities for growth and development
(RESEARCH?)		• identify opportunities for growth and development • attend library meetings and industry events, as required
OTHER: • Bachelor's degree, preferably in a biological science. • domestic and international travel is required.		

After completing the "You" and "Us" portions of this chart, applicants would then review their résumés and other job-related materials for "proof" (that is, specific experiences and training that demonstrate the skills the company wants in the employee it hires). They would then plug that information into the middle column of the Brainstorming Chart, next to the corresponding qualification or skill. For example:

"YOU" Wish-List of Characteristics	"ME" "Proof" you have the characteristic	"US" Transferability Factor
LEADERSHIP: • demonstrated ability to manage and train staff.	• identified operational demands, delegated tasks, monitored team members' progress • led quarterly product sales training	• manage and train Journal Sales Executive and supporting staff

As you review these examples, know that there is no "right" way to complete the "You–Me–Us Brainstorming Chart." In fact, depending on your particular training and interests, you could group details from the job announcement in different ways to streamline discussions or to emphasize (or downplay) particular expectations.

Also know that, while completing the "You" and "Us" portions of this chart may be easier with a job announcement in hand, you could use this chart to generate information for unsolicited applications, too. The difference is that for unsolicited applications, *you* would need to identify and fill in the "Wish-List of Characteristics" your target company would expect in prospective employees (i.e., the "You" column); you must also provide the "Transferability" factors for those characteristics (i.e., the "Us" column). Here's one reason that knowing about the industry in general and the company in particular would be invaluable.

Regardless of whether you apply for solicited or unsolicited positions, you should complete a You–Me–Us Brainstorming Chart for *each* company that interests you. That task may seem time-intensive, but comparable positions within a single industry will have details that inevitably overlap; therefore, completing one chart will make it easier to complete Brainstorming Charts for other companies. Furthermore, as you create charts for each company that appeals to you, you may begin to see differences between and among each company's portrayal of the specific position; for example, you may find differences in the tasks you'd be asked to do, the goals you would support, the procedures you could use, the products you might promote, the clients you would serve, or the results you'd be accountable for depending on the particular organization.

By understanding how a given job title or position might be represented and performed across an industry, you can identify and prioritize organizations to pursue. You would also be able to discuss a specific position and its requirements in more knowledgeable ways, such as during an interview or salary negations.

For now, however, we will examine how the information in a You–Me–Us Brainstorming Chart can help you create application letters that stand out to hiring managers, and the following exercise can get you started.

Exercise: Creating a You–Me–Us Brainstorming Chart

For this exercise, you will need a copy of the You–Me–Us Brainstorming Chart (see following pages) and a print out of the job announcement for a position you'd like to apply to in the near future. You may also want to have on hand a copy of your résumé(s), and other job application materials you have generated.

Step 1. List the specific requirements, expectations, qualifications and so forth from the company's job announcement in the first column, "You."

Step 2. List training and experience you could offer the company as "proof" that you meet each particular requirement, expectation, qualification… in the second column, "Me," next to the company's corresponding "Wish List" entry. For ideas, you might refer to your résumé and other application materials you have generated—even those you may no longer be using.

Step 3. Indicate where, how, and to what extent your general, industry-oriented training could be put to use in this specific organization, given its place in the field or industry, as well as its culture, clients, products, services, and values… in the third column, "Us." This information might be ascertained from the job description itself, as well as from discussions with recruiters and company representatives, the company's website, or other materials you have about the organization.

You–Me–Us Brainstorming Chart

Company Name and Address:		
Position and, if available, reference number:		
Where/How learned about position:		
"You" **Wish-List of Characteristics** Here, insert applicant qualifications called out in the company's job announcement	**"ME"** **"Proof" you have characteristic s** Here, list the specific positions, activities, training, experiences, degrees, classes and workshops, and other tangible practices demonstrating you have the desired characteristic or skill (consult your résumé and other application materials for ideas)	**"US"** **Transferability Factor** Here, identify ways you could use or apply this skill in the target company's construction of the position; incorporate details you acquired by researching the company, networking…

"You" Wish-List of Characteristics (continued)	"ME" "Proof" you have characteristic s (continued)	"US" Transferability Factor (continued)

While plugging details into these columns, you may discover information that falls into one or more columns, giving you options of where and how to best address those details. You might also discover that some details overlap with, or even duplicate other information. In such cases, you could group several elements under a single, larger characteristic or skill, indicating the relationships you see between and among particular information.

* * *

Once you complete this chart, you're in a position to write the main paragraphs for your application letter, using the "You–Me–Us" structure to highlight your qualifications for employment.

Echoing the Principle of Burying, the "You–Me–Us" paragraph structure starts and ends each paragraph with information that is of greatest interest to the reader, burying information that is important, but of less interest, in the middle. For application letters, then, paragraphs should begin and end with information of greatest interest to the hiring manager and downplay, or bury, information about applicant.

The "You–Me–Us" Paragraph Structure, Overview

Topic Sentence Reader's attention is HIGH	**"YOU"** Particular skill/ability/trait… the company asks for in its advertisement or, if an unsolicited application, a skill/ability/trait… that would be expected or desired in the target company's employees
Middle Sentence(s) Reader's attention may be minimal or sporadic	**"Me"** "Proof" that you have that skill/ability/trait…
Closing Sentence(s) Reader's attention is HIGH	**"Us"** Ability to transfer skill/ability/trait… to the reader's specific organization

The information from your "You–Me–Us Brainstorming Chart" will help you fill in the particular details.

Topic Sentence

To begin with information that's of greatest interest to a hiring manager, your topic sentences should focus on a particular feature or skill the company requests in the advertisement—information you transcribed in the first column of the Brainstorming Chart, the "You" column.

For solicited positions, most of this information will come from the job announcement, but you could also use details from the company's website or references to conversations you may have had with a company representative, say at a job fair or during an earlier informational interview. In fact, doing so can be advantageous, suggesting you have researched the company or otherwise invested time in learning about the organization—an action that speaks well of applicants wanting a position with the particular company.

Sample topic sentences highlighting something from the company's Wish List include:

> **Example 1**
>
> Your advertisement notes you are looking for someone who can write code for portability across platforms, and my background developing client server applications that have run on the Windows, Linux, Android and iPhone platforms have given me skills I can use to help your division build mission critical software.
>
> **Example 2**
>
> During our conversation, you said that you were most interested in applicants who can oversee several projects simultaneously; my experience managing 8–10 client portfolios at Industrial Angel Designs has prepared me for such work.

By focusing on a single "wish" in each topic sentence—rather than listing everything the organization may want in an applicant—you establish a context for discussing aspects of your training in greater depth, but in ways a hiring manager would value.

Middle Sentence(s)

Having identified a characteristic or skill of interest to the hiring manager, you would then explain the training and experience that demonstrates where and how you have developed that characteristic or skill, drawing upon the information that appears in the second column of your Brainstorming Chart, the "Me" column.

Typically, this information would come from your résumé, but it's also possible to include details that are not on your résumé—either because they didn't fit or because the information may not be appropriate in all forums in which your résumé circulates. For example, someone applying for positions in publishing might not indicate a passion for gardening on the résumé, but that detail could be appropriate to mention in an application letter to a gardening magazine looking for an editor.

Because it may not be possible to present all of the experience you have with a particular skill, the sentences in your application letter should focus on the skills, training, projects, positions, companies, and so on that would be of greatest interest to the particular company, demonstrating your awareness of its practices and values.

Closing Sentence(s)

The final step is to write a sentence or two that ends the paragraph explaining how you could transfer your experiences to help the hiring manager and the larger company meet their specific goals.

Drawing upon the information that appears in the third column of your Brainstorming Chart, the "Us" column, these sentences might note where and how you could apply the training and experience you acquired in other forums to satisfy a requirement mentioned in the job announcement. Or, you might explain how your experiences have prepared you to contribute to a particular project or effort you learned about through the company's website or in conversations you had with company employees. Similarly, you might note how your experiences can help you uphold company values and ideals, or particular elements of the company's philosophy or mission statement. This "transferability" information helps hiring managers envision you working within their company in like-minded ways.

To demonstrate how application letters might bring all of these elements together, consider the following paragraphs, which apply the You-Me-Us structure.

Example:

Details from a *single* paragraph, with sentences separated to highlight information in each segment of the "You–Me–Us" structure

"YOU" Your advertisement notes that the applicant for Detrio's Product Help-Line Manager should have strong communication abilities, and the work I do for Zangram Associates has helped me hone my speaking and writing abilities.

"ME" For example, each week I generate pitches that document product specifications and benefits to prospective clients. Understanding that our clients first learn about Zangram products through secondary vendors, I ensure the product literature I review with current distributors, as well as the materials I present at sales conventions and use during on-site demonstrations, are comprehensible to prospective representatives and their team members. I then call vendors and representatives every 1–2 months to discuss how products are meeting their expectations, address their questions and concerns, and promote products in the production pipeline that may be of interest.

"US" Such experience will help me answer questions about Detrio's products and services for colleagues and customers who may be unfamiliar with engineering terminology. My participation in Toastmasters will further ensure that I can accurately describe Detrio's products to customers who call the company for assistance.

The start of another paragraph

"YOU" Working with teams of 2–8 people has also given me teamwork experience your advertisement says applicants should possess.

"ME" As the point person for a team that was exploring new audiences for one of our computer modules, I have learned to introduce, support, critique, and negotiate ideas with team members in ways that encourage each member to contribute information while simultaneously allowing the team to assess and build upon the most appropriate ideas for the task at hand.

"US" At Detrio, I could use these teamwork skills to…

Now that you have seen the You–Me–Us structure in action, it's your turn to use this structure to write paragraphs for your own application letter.

Exercise: Generating "You–Me–Us" Paragraphs

To generate reader-oriented paragraphs that might appear in your application letter, you will need the "You–Me–Us Brainstorming Chart" you completed in the previous exercise.

Step 1. Select one item from the company's Wish List (the "You" column) that you could satisfy or, if writing an unsolicited application letter, identify one characteristic or skill that's common to employees doing the work you'd like to do for this company. As noted earlier, if there is overlap in items that appear on the company's Wish-List, you might consider combining and condensing the entries under a single, larger characteristic or trait.

Company's Wish List Item: ______________________________

Step 2. Write a topic sentence that identifies the "wish" you can fulfill and where you learned about that wish, starting the discussion with the *hiring manager's* need or interest. Sample sentence structures include:

> Your advertisement notes you are looking for applicants who can ____________, and I offer ____.
>
> During our conversation, you said that you were most interested in applicants who had experience in_______________; my position at _______________ has prepared me for this work.
>
> Talking with one of your representatives at __________, I learned that my training in ______ could help your company ________________.
>
> Visiting your website, I noticed that your company values _________, and my work on _____________ would allow me to uphold these views.

Your Sentence:

Step 3. Write 2–3 sentences to explain the background, training, and experience you have verifying that you can satisfy that particular Wish. For these sentences, incorporate details from the "Me" column of your You–Me–Us Brainstorming Chart, as well as information from other application materials that demonstrate you have the particular skill, experience, or expertise you identify in Step 2. In writing about this training and experience, briefly explain *what* you did, *how* you did it, and the *short- and long-term impact your efforts had*. In doing so, promote details this specific company would value.

Step 4. Write a sentence or two that explains how you could *transfer* the experience, training, background… you wrote about in Step 3 to the specific reader's organization. Here, elaborate on the information in the "Us" column of your You–Me–Us Brainstorming Chart, explaining where and how you might be able to apply and build upon your present abilities to meet a goal mentioned in the job announcement, to contribute to a company-specific project, or to uphold larger company values and ideals.

Once you've completed this process for one item from the company's Wish List, complete the process for 1–2 more "wishes" the company may value most in a preliminary review of job applicant materials.

Secret 19: Too much hype and too little substance make applicants seem insecure, or even desperate.

As noted earlier, relative terms affect both résumés and application letters, but in different ways. When relative terms appear in a résumé, readers may be able to use contextual details (e.g., industry, organization, position, job description information) to identify and authenticate an applicant's qualifications despite any hyperbolic language. When application letters use relative terms, however, it's often at the expense of contextualizing details; in other words, job applicants assume that the relative terms are sufficient for conveying both their abilities and their degree of competence, as evident in the following, representative excerpts from application letters in various industries:

> I am highly motivated, friendly and personable.
>
> I am a fast learner, able to master complex details quickly with minimal supervision.
>
> I have diverse experience in customer service and extensive leadership experience, which I can use to make valuable contributions to your company.
>
> My experiences have given me exceptional experience in sales.
>
> I am eager to apply my wide-ranging training and skills in your firm.
>
> I am very interested in working for your firm. I bring excellent communication skills and strong team work.

Each of these sentences contains one or more relative terms—adjectives and concepts that assume *identical* points of reference for defining, gauging, and understanding what *highly motivated*, *friendly*, *personable*, and so on means in a particular context:

> I am **highly motivated**, **friendly** and **personable**.
>
> I am a **fast** learner, able to master **complex** details **quickly** with **minimal** supervision.
>
> I have **diverse** experience in customer service and **extensive** leadership experience, which I can use to make **valuable** contributions to your company.
>
> My experiences have given me **exceptional** experience in sales.
>
> I am **eager** to apply my **wide-ranging** training and skills in your firm.
>
> I am **very interested** in working for your firm. I bring **excellent** communication skills and **strong** team work.

Applicants may know what *they* mean when they use such words, and hiring managers may know what *they* mean when they see or hear these words, but it's unclear whether applicants and hiring managers mean *exactly* the same thing.

Running through the "*X* was so *Y*" trope and the reporter's "The Five Ws" and the question "How?" explained in Secret 9, we can better understand the concerns a hiring manager might have about the applicant's professed expertise. "Highly motivated" according to what standards? "Friendly" by whose definition? "Personable" in what forum? What constitutes "complex details," how "quickly" were they learned, and what kind of supervision is deemed "minimal"?

Such questions, left unanswered, make it harder for hiring managers to gauge what an applicant has done and, more importantly, what the applicant can do for their company, especially since claiming competency doesn't make it so. By revising sentences in ways that replace relative terms with concrete, non-disputable details, applicants can clarify *what* they did, *when*, *how*, *for whom*, and the *results* of those efforts, thereby helping hiring managers understand their credentials, as the following revisions demonstrate:

> **Original**
> I am a fast learner, able to master complex details quickly with minimal supervision.

Revision, Example 1

Although my position did not require me to work with AutoCAD, I completed online tutorials to familiarize myself with the program and, within two months, I was using the program to incorporate client specifications into a senior partner's designs and to draft preliminary architectural drawings for pitch meetings.

Revision, Example 2

Because the West Coast office did not have conventional staffing, as an entry-level analyst I had the opportunity to assume responsibilities typically reserved for Associates and Vice Presidents. Therefore, in addition to researching industries, building models, and preparing pitch books, I provided project updates during weekly team member calls, represented our group at out-of-town client meetings, scheduled administrative and industry group staff members throughout deal offerings, and fielded team leader and client calls during deal offering development.

Revision, Example 3

In November 2014, I joined LuxCom as a mid-level sales associate, selling modular systems to corporations and individuals. In October 2015, I was promoted to Sales Manager, overseeing 12 representatives covering the company's Midwest Division. In addition to assigning territories, establishing individual representative and larger division sales targets, and running monthly training programs for the team, I have attended company-sponsored sales training seminars every year and have participated in SMEI's national marketing programs, learning skills that have helped my team increase sales in LuxCom's technology division by 7% in two years.

Moving from descriptions like the original to any of the possible revisions will take time, but that time is worth it, for the following reasons.

First, with practice, you will become more familiar with the type of information to include in your application letters, making you more sensitive to the ways you think about and describe the work you do to hiring managers. Second, you will have and retain greater control over the expectations people have for you and, by extension, the ways you're positioned in the market; after all, hiring managers will not need to guess or infer what you may be able to do, since you have explicitly identified what you *can* do. Third, considering that few job applicants take the time to offer concrete explanations, your materials will begin to stand out from the rest, generating interviews in even the toughest economy. Finally, even modest changes can shift a hiring manager's understanding of what you can do, ensuring a better match between you and the work you're hired to do.

Even for those who recognize the benefits, writing sentences that contain tangible, non-negotiable details can still be intimidating. Therefore, the following exercise offers strategies for finding and replacing the relative terms in your application letter with information that stands out to hiring managers.

Exercise: Application Letter Show or Tell?

This activity focuses on conveying what you do—or what you have done—to those who may not have first-hand knowledge of the work you have performed. For this exercise, you will need a hard copy of your application letter. If you would like additional space to make comments and editorial notations, you might consider double spacing your letter before printing it.

Step 1. Highlight the relative terms (adjectives, adverbs, concepts) that assume identical points of reference.

Step 2. Ask yourself, "What information do *readers* need to understand what I did, as I did it, in the forum(s) in which I did it with the resources I had at my disposal?" for *each* element you highlighted.

To help generate information that might appear in a revised description, use the "*X* was so *Y*" trope to identify details that could answer the question "How *Y* was it?" Or, use conventional reporter questions (Who? What? Where? When? Why? How?), adding "So what?" to identify short- and long-term effects of the work you did.

Step 3. Answer each question with concrete, tangible details (e.g., dollar figures, percentages, numbers, ranges, software programs, industry protocols, actions, sequence of actions), one description at a time.

Step 4. Revise each highlighted application letter entry to incorporate your answers into the descriptions.

In moving through these steps, your explanations and, by extension, your application letter will become longer, but you should resist censoring yourself *at this stage*. For now, focus on providing the most complete and accurate information to help the hiring manager understand the work as *you* performed it.

Once you have clarified what you have done, you will be able to identify which information this hiring manager needs to know to call you in for an interview, and which information might be best presented during the actual interview. Using that information, you can then condense and tighten the details in the application letter you ultimately submit.

Secret 20: A concise, action-oriented closing paragraph demonstrates your interest in—and hunger for—the position.

After spending one or more paragraphs explaining how and why they are a match for the position, job applicants should end their letter on a positive, action-oriented note. Unfortunately, most application letters end with passive, wishy-washy sentiments such as, "If you'd like to hear more about my qualifications, please call me at your earliest convenience" or "Thank you in advance for your consideration."

Such closings present the applicant as someone who is content to sit back and wait for job opportunities to come to them but, in tight job markets, opportunities often go to the individuals who can both make a case for employment *and* go after prospects in professionally assertive ways. Therefore the way you close your application letter can make the difference between securing an interview, or not.

To wrap up your letter and stand out from the competition, your application letter's closing paragraph should do several things, as outlined below.

Mention enclosed (or attached) résumé

Some application letters mention the enclosed (or attached) résumé in the opening paragraph; some letters mention the résumé in the middle paragraphs; some mention it in the closing paragraph; some mention it in an enclosure notation, such as "Encl: Résumé"; some letters mention the résumé in all four places; and others don't mention the résumé at all, assuming its enclosure or attachment is self-evident. Yet the most strategic place to mention the résumé is the *closing* paragraph. Here's why.

Mentioning an enclosed document at any time before the last paragraph encourages readers to redirect their attention elsewhere, often at the expense of the present discussion. For example, application letters that begin, "As my enclosed résumé indicates…," prompt hiring managers to put down the application letter and pick up the résumé. In such cases, the two pages the applicant did have to make a case for employment (i.e., an industry-specific résumé *and* a company-specific application letter), now becomes a single page: the résumé.

Mentioning the résumé in a body paragraph has a similar effect; it prematurely redirects the hiring manager's attention elsewhere.

Of course hiring managers could turn their attention immediately to the résumé upon opening the envelope or computer file. The difference is that you, the applicant, are not explicitly directing the reader to look elsewhere. By waiting until the last paragraph to mention the résumé, you have a better chance of keeping the hiring manager's eyes on the letter that explains why *you're* qualified for *this* particular position. Therefore, with one exception, you should plan to reference your résumé in the last paragraph of your application letter.

The exception to this guideline is when you are following up on an earlier conversation in which the hiring manager has explicitly asked you to forward your résumé. In this case, you would mention your résumé in the opening paragraph. For example:

> Thank you for talking with me at the Alonex Software Developer Job Fair on June 23, 20XX, about opportunities in your company. As requested, I am sending along a copy of my résumé.

Such openings are strategic for several reasons. First, by reminding the reader of your earlier discussion, you indirectly suggest you have been vetted, even briefly, standing apart from those responding to a generic job announcement. Second, by noting that you're following up on the reader's request—to send along a résumé—you demonstrate that you can follow through on a task without needing to write, "I can follow through on tasks."

Finally, such openings help extend earlier conversations. For instance, by using the You–Me–Us paragraph structure, you could use details from your conversation with the reader to focus your application letter's body paragraphs. In doing do, you show that you were paying attention to what that person said and, by extension, reinforce your awareness of that person's needs and interests, as the opening lines of the following body paragraph demonstrate:

> During our conversation, you mentioned that DigitCorp values applicants with experience in both conventional and new programming languages; my coursework at Louisiana Tech University, as well as my industry experiences, have given me theoretical and hands-on experience with languages on Linux, Microsoft Windows, and Mac OS platforms, which I could bring to projects similar to those you mentioned. For example…"

In cases where you mention the résumé in the opening paragraph of your application letter, you do not need to mention the résumé again in the closing paragraph; in fact, doing so would be repetitious. The closing paragraph in this case would pick up on other details that should appear in an application letter's final paragraph.

Ask for "Interview"

In their effort to distinguish themselves from the competition, some applicants use words other than "interview," writing things like, "I would welcome the opportunity to talk with you further about this position." Or, "I would be happy to meet to discuss what I could bring to your organization." The problem with these and comparable phrases is that they suggest the person writing the letter may be interested in something other than employment, say, an informational interview.

By using the word "interview," you clarify that you are applying for a job. Therefore, use the word "interview" in your closing paragraph—unless, of course, you *are* seeking an informational interview to learn more about the industry, the company, positions the company often has available, skills applicants must demonstrate, and so on in order to strengthen your application when you are, in fact, on the market.

Note you will call in 7–10 days, and be sure to follow up

Many job applicants claim they are energetic, eager, up-to-the challenge kind of people who take the initiative to go after what they want, and yet most application letters end on a note that suggests otherwise. Phrases such as, "If you would like to talk further, please call me" depict applicants who assume hiring managers will pursue them, even though hiring managers are not the ones looking for a position.

Therefore, by taking a professional, proactive approach to employment, you can increase your chances of securing an interview. The following sentences demonstrate this principle in action:

> **Example 1**
> Enclosed is a copy of my résumé offering further details of my qualifications. I will call your office in 7–10 days to arrange an interview for the sales manager position.
>
> **Example 2**
> Enclosed is my résumé, and I will call your office in 7–10 days to confirm you have received my application.

Such sentences may seem presumptuous, and in some ways they are. But, considering you've just spent the last several paragraphs explaining how you are a solid match for *this* position, not just *a* position, you're less presumptuous than applicants who say they'll call without having demonstrated an awareness of the company or its needs. In the context of a reader-specific, You–Me–Us application letter, you're simply taking the next, logical step—that is, to meet with those in the organization—and you're making it easier for the reader by initiating the call. This strategy, however, comes with some caveats.

First, telling the reader that you will call in 7–10 days is not permission to hound or harass a hiring manager; rather, it is an indication that you will follow-up on whether your application has arrived, giving you an opportunity to gauge whether further conversation about the position is possible at this time, or at all. Furthermore, noting that you will call in 7–10 days when the job announcement explicitly indicates "no calls" indicates you are unable to follow directions, so you should confirm whether calls are feasible before making this offer.

You should also have (or verify that you can find) the reader's phone number—or at least a number that is more direct than the corporate office's general directory—so you can call and, if necessary, leave a message for the reader. If phone numbers are unavailable, or if most correspondence for the position is done online, alternative phrasing for your follow-up sentence may be, "I will e-mail you in 7–10 days to confirm you have received my application." You are still being proactive but, for some readers, less intrusive.

Perhaps the most important consideration for this strategy is that you must follow up. To say you will call in 7–10 days and then blow off the call suggests that you're using job applicant gimmicks or, worse, that you don't keep your word.

Give information on how to reach you if the hiring manager has questions in the meantime

Even when applicants note they will be calling the company in the coming days, prospective employers may need more information before that call. Therefore, you should include a phone number and email address in your application letter's closing paragraph, with the following considerations.

First, you should provide a phone number and email address that offers the most immediate and direct access to you; offering phone numbers you seldom use, voicemails you hardly check, and email addresses you don't consult will not reflect favorably on you and your application if a hiring manager cannot reach you with the information you've provided.

That said, you should offer a phone number and email address that allows you and the hiring manager to discuss job opportunities without reservation; that is, resist giving your work phone number and e-mail address during a job search, especially if your current employer does not know you're looking for another position.

Finally, you should be attentive to hidden messages your contact information may give prospective employers. Outgoing voicemail messages, for example, can reveal phone skills in a professional context, while email addresses may offer details a hiring manager can use against you (e.g., beerlover@gmail.com, ratherbesleeping@aol.com, sexyback@gmail.com, imathrillseeker@yahoo.com). By ensuring that your contact information will help you convey and reinforce a professional image, you can enhance the case you make for employment.

* * *

The following examples show how an application letter's closing paragraph might bring together all of these elements into a few sentences:

> **Example 1**
>
> Enclosed is my résumé, and I will call you in 7–10 days to schedule

an interview. If, in the meantime, you have questions, please call me at 415-555-1212, or email me at jdoe@gmail.com. Thank you.

Example 2

As requested, I am enclosing my résumé, writing samples, and the names of two references, and I will call in 7–10 days to confirm that you have received these materials. Meanwhile, if you have questions about these items or need additional information, please call me at 202-555-1212, or email me at jdoe@gmail.com. I look forward to meeting you. Thank you.

One final note about the closing paragraph. Saying thank you at the end is a professional courtesy, but often applicants misidentify what they are thanking readers for. Some applicants write, for example, “Thank you for your consideration,” presuming they are, in fact, being considered when the hiring manager may have stopped reading the letter after the opening paragraph—or earlier. Other application letters end with, “Thanking you in advance,” suggesting that the applicant cannot be bothered to thank the hiring manager at a later point.

To end of application letter politely and professionally, “Thank you” is sufficient.

Exercise: Creating a Concise, Action-Oriented Closing Paragraph

This exercise guides you through the steps of ending your application letter with precision and professional good will.

Step 1. Identify the best place to mention your résumé in this letter, based on any earlier interactions you may have had with the hiring manager:

- ❑ In the *Closing* Paragraph
- ❑ In the *Opening* Paragraph, if following up on an earlier interaction

Step 2. Identify the next immediate exchange you want to occur because of this letter

- ❑ *Interview*, for employment
- ❑ *Informational interview*, to gather more information prior to applying for employment

Step 3. Ensure that you could call or email the hiring manager in 7–10 days to verify receipt of your application materials by confirming:

- ❑ The job announcement does not say "no calls," or something comparable
- ❑ You have the hiring manager's phone number and/or email address:

  Hiring manager's phone number and extension:

  ____

  Hiring manager's email address:

  ____

Step 4. Identify the most direct and immediate ways this company could reach ***you***, ensuring those options are those you check frequently, as well as those that would give you the opportunity to communicate with prospective employers without worrying about others (e.g., company administrators, supervisors, coworkers) who may have access to those forums.

- ❏ phone number: ______________________________
- ❏ email address: ______________________________

Using the information you recorded in the previous steps, write a 1–2 sentence paragraph that will close your application letter in a concise, proactive manner.

____

____

____

____

____

____

____

____

____

____

____

____

____

Step 5. Prepare to follow up on your application by identifying a tentative date(s) you should plan to call or email the reader, based on 7–10 days from the time you mail or otherwise submit your application.

- ❑ Tentative follow up date(s): ______________________

Your letter should *not* mention this date in the closing paragraph because you, or the hiring manager, may not be available on the date you mention. Rather, you are documenting the date(s) you should follow up to commit yourself to being in a place that would allow you to talk with the hiring manager, or at least leave a message with minimal distraction.

Exercise: Bringing It All Together

The last few exercises helped you create segments of the You–Me–Us application letter. Now it's time to bring these pieces together into a single, cohesive letter that explains why you are qualified for the position in a way that appeals to hiring managers.

Step 1. Copy and paste the elements from the previous exercises into a single document, making sure your letter includes the following elements:

- ❑ Salutation
- ❑ Company-specific opening paragraph
- ❑ You–Me–Us internal paragraphs
- ❑ Concise, action-oriented closing paragraph

Step 2. Review the letter for cohesion, clarity, and grammatical accuracy, editing as necessary to meet the conventional one-page limit.

Step 3. Run the spell checker, recognizing that spell checkers do not catch everything.

Step 4. Print two copies of the document.

Step 5. Ask someone to read your letter aloud—exactly as it is written—as you follow along with the second copy, noting areas the reader stumbles, struggles, or otherwise has difficulty moving through the document.

Step 6. Revise the document to address the reader's concerns, as well as other elements you may have noticed when hearing your document read aloud.

Final Notes...

You could spend countless hours churning out hundreds of application materials for companies that, ultimately, may be of little interest, or you could spend that time researching companies that seem like places you'd like to work and generate company-specific application materials to 4–5 organizations that offer the best match for your talents and interests.

Statistically, both approaches would generate the same return: a handful of interviews. Yet by researching and evaluating companies that interest you up front, you develop a richer understanding of the how the work you'd like to do may be situated within and constructed by a particular company—and across industries—and this information can be invaluable as you compare job opportunities, applicant expectations, and position requirements. This information could also help you prepare for interviews and create a stronger position from which to negotiate job offers.

* * *

May you always have work that engages and inspires you, and a forum to do that work for or alongside those who will appreciate your contribution.

Exercise: The $50k Investment Test

It is one thing to ask a company to pay its employees for the work they do on the organization's behalf, but it is another thing for *employees* to pay the organization for the opportunity to do that work. And yet employees *do* pay their employers. Granted, they may not be writing out checks, but employees are investing in their employers with the energy they spend, the materials they produce, the products they sell, the ideas they offer, the clients they secure… all contributing to the company's brand and bottom line. The question then becomes whether employees are investing their resources in the ways or in the forums they value.

Assume you had $50,000 (or the annual salary your profession supports) to invest in a *single* company for one year. Would you trust your current employer—or a company you'd like to work for—with that *entire* investment? For example, would you write a personal check to the company's CEO? Would you buy stock in the company as it is presently configured or managed? Would you invest in the research and development of the organization's products and services, or actually purchase the results of those efforts? Would you financially subsidize work the organization does, the values it espouses, the direction it's heading, the reputation it holds, the leadership it offers, and the systems it maintains?

By understanding where you would invest the resources *you* can offer, you can identify organizations that could both benefit from your contributions and help you achieve the returns you seek from your investment.

About the Author

Caroline M. Cole maintains that business is about mutually rewarding relationships and that such relationships are built and sustained with genuine interactions. For over 25 years, she has focused on the ways written and oral communication practices can help in those endeavors.

A native of Chicago, Caroline earned a B.A. in English and Rhetoric, an M.Ed. in Curriculum & Instruction, and a Ph.D. in Writing Studies from the University of Illinois at Urbana-Champaign. As a faculty member at the University of California, Berkeley, Caroline has taught written and oral communication for College Writing Programs and the Walter A. Haas School of Business. Over the years, her audiences have grown to include undergraduate and graduate students regardless of disciplinary interests or career paths.

After years of talking with industry professionals about the shortage of communication resources and opportunities available to them, she founded Ethos Professional Communication in 2003, offering seminars, workshops, and consulting services to promote communication practices that value and reward all participants. Although her attention has expanded to include industry professionals, Caroline's on-going work at the university allows her to research the latest communication theories and practices. By engaging in both university and workplace forums, she works to bridge the gap between academic training and industry expectations.

Caroline remains committed to helping others present their ideas, their products and services, and themselves in the best possible manner. To learn more, please visit www.ethosprofessionalcommunication.com

www.ingramcontent.com/pod-product-compliance
Lightning Source LLC
Chambersburg PA
CBHW051411200326
41520CB00023B/7192
9780998138701